NTURES IN MOTION PICTURES • ... • ALAN PRICE • ALEXEI SAYLE
NLON • ARE YOU LONESOME TONIG... , THE SHEEP PIG • BARBARA DICKSON
HE BEATLES • THE BEE GEES • BEN E KING • BEN ELTON • BILLY CONNOLLY • BILLY
OOD BROTHERS • THE BLUE JAYS • BOBBY DAVRO • THE BOLSHOI BALLET • BOTTOM
• CABARET • CANNON & BALL • CARMEN JONES • THE CARPENTERS • CAT STEVENS
ARLIE AND THE CHOCOLATE FACTORY • CHARLIE GIRL • CHAR... WILLIAMS • CHER
ERRY • THE CLANCY BROTHERS • CLANNAD • CLEO LAINE • C... • CLIVE
AME EDNA EVERAGE • DANNY LA RUE • DAVE ALLEN • DAVID ... ONNOR
• DORIS COLLINS • DOROTHY SQUIRES • THE DRIFTERS • THE ... • DUKE
OUSINS • ELKIE BROOKS • ELVIS – THE MUSICAL • EMMA THOMPSON • ENGELBERT
N THE ROOF • FIREMAN SAM • FIVE GUYS NAMED MOE • THE FLYING PICKETS • THE
GHAN • FREDDIE STARR • FRENCH & SAUNDERS • THE GANG SHOW • GENE PITNEY
E GINGERBREAD MAN • GO AND PLAY UP YOUR OWN END • GODSPELL • THE GOOD
JONES & MEL SMITH • GUYS & DOLLS • HAIR • HALE & PACE • HAPPY DAYS • HARRY
ALPERT • HIGH SOCIETY • HINGE AND BRACKETT • THE HOLLIES • HOT CHOCOLATE
• JASPER CARROT • JERRY LEE LEWIS • JESUS CHRIST SUPERSTAR • JIM BAILEY • JIM
EN HANSON • JOHNNY CASH SHOW • JOHNNY MATHIS • JOLSON • JOSE FELICIANO
• KENNY ROGERS • KISS ME KATE • KRIS KRISTOFFERSON AND RITA COOLIDGE • LA
• LES MISERABLES • LINDISFARNE • LONDON CONTEMPORARY DANCE • LOU REED
ETRICH • MARTI WEBB • MARTIN GUERRE • MAX BOYCE • MAX BYGRAVES • ME & MY
RECAMBE & WISE • MUD • THE MUPPETS • MY FAIR LADY • NANA MOUSKOURI • NEIL
NLY THE LONELY • OPERA NORTH • OTIS REDDING • OWL & PUSSYCAT • PADDINGTON
UL MCCARTNEY & WINGS • PAUL SIMON • PETULA CLARK • THE PHANTOM OF THE
E MUSICAL • RAB C NESBITT • RALPH MCTELL • RANDY CRAWFORD • RAVI SHANKAR
HORROR SHOW • THE ROLLING STONES • RORY BREMNER • ROSIE & JIM • ROWAN
S ABBOT • SAMMY DAVIS • SANTANA • SESAME STREET • SEVEN BRIDES FOR SEVEN
EL • SINGIN' IN THE RAIN • S... SNOOPY – THE MUSICAL • SOME
N • STEELEYE SPAN • STEE... SONDHEIM • TAMMY WYNETTE
REES • THEY'RE PLAYING OU... BIRDS • TOMMY STEELE • TONY
VICTOR BORGE • VICTORIA WOOD • WAYNE SLEEP • THE WHO • THE WITCHES

BIRMINGHAM HIPPODROME

1899-1999

Fred Norris

Published by
© Birmingham Hippodrome Theatre Trust Limited
Hurst Street, Birmingham B5 4TB, United Kingdom

British Library Cataloguing-in-Publication Data
A catalogue record for this book is available from The British Library

ISBN 0 9537292 0 6 *hardback*

First published 1999

Designed by Lionart, Birmingham
Printed by Menzies Nunn, Brierley Hill, West Midlands
Bound by Hunter and Foulis, Edinburgh

In 1990, when Birmingham Royal Ballet was established, Sir Peter Wright created a new production of 'The Nutcracker' and dedicated it to the City that had given the company a new home. Sets and costumes by John Macfarlane. Lighting by David A. Finn.
Photo by Bill Cooper.

To Angie who, with near-divine patience and a tolerance that defies measure, has endured a lifetime of the late nights, early mornings and prolonged absences that are the daily hazards of marriage to a newspaper man and theatre critic.

I would like to thank Martin Cinnamond, Vanessa Rawlings-Jackson, Mandy Price and particularly Judith Cartwright for the additional research material.

As a journalist, archives are always an important resource, and in compiling this history the assistance given by the Birmingham Post & Mail and the Local Studies & History Service in Birmingham Central Library has been invaluable.

I am most appreciative for the text written by Anne Sacks, Dance Critic of the London Evening Standard, on Birmingham Royal Ballet, and also to Simon Rees, Dramaturg of the Welsh National Opera for their contributions.

Photography captures the moment and memory of the theatrical performance, and I am grateful to Bill Cooper and Alan Wood for their kind permission to reproduce much of their work in this book.

Fred Norris
November 1999

Foreword by Cameron Mackintosh

This book has two reasons for celebration: first, the triumphant survival of the Birmingham Hippodrome through the ups and downs of this last century which has seen so much change; and secondly, the tireless enthusiasm of the author of this fascinating record, Fred Norris, who seems to have been a pivotal and influential figure of Birmingham theatre for almost as long as the hundred years of the Hippodrome itself!

Newspaper and theatre tastes have changed considerably over the years, and wherever I travel in the world, the particular local or regional paper is one of the first things I ask for (and often a translator!). The tradition and importance of a newspaper's regular theatre critic is something, as a producer taking a show "out of town", that I particularly care about. Sadly, very few cities can these days boast of a seasoned, informed critic. Reviewing is usually now just part of the duties of a reporter delegated to doing showbiz features. Birmingham has always been an exception in this regard, a proud beacon of high quality theatrical criticism respected both locally and nationally, including Kenneth Tynan and J.C. Trewin both of whom wrote authoritative reviews and, of course, Fred Norris himself for so many decades on the Evening Mail. Whether or not Fred has liked a production, he has always commanded the respect of the theatrical profession. He is that rare critic who always goes into the theatre looking to write about a great evening, and taking no pleasure in reporting a failure. His affection for theatre is one of the reasons why it is so appropriate that he has lovingly woven together the rich tapestry of the Hippodrome's own history.

The first time I played the Birmingham Hippodrome was as a young actor in 1966 with *Oliver!* when I played a hyperactive London pot boy, outrageously over-acting in the crowd scenes. My first production on the Hippodrome's vast stage was a disastrously sparse and tacky production of *Little Women*. In recent years I've tried a bit harder with my productions of *Cats*, *Les Misérables* and, most recently, *The Phantom of the Opera* which did marginally better playing to 199,529 patrons in a capacity season! The national production of the musical *Miss Saigon* opens at the newly refurbished Hippodrome in 2001 and my production team is already preparing for this great spectacular after its sensational ten long years' run at the Theatre Royal, Drury Lane.

Julian Slade, who influenced the destiny of my own career with his enchanting musical *Salad Days,* included the song "I'll ask you to remind me, to say we will never look back". This book is the exception! You are now invited to reminisce through the decades, performances and shows of the Hippodrome's colourful past, and I hope they bring back very happy memories of theatregoing at the Hippodrome and make you look forward to an even richer future.

November 1999

Reflections

Fred Norris shares his personal reflections on the changing phases in the life of the Hippodrome – from sawdust to high opera and ballet

LIKE MOST people my first introduction to the wonders of theatre, and an association with the Birmingham Hippodrome spanning nearly half a century, was a pantomime. I have to this day memories of Arthur Askey swinging about in the basket of what was supposed to be a hot-air balloon – yes, Arthur got into one long before Richard Branson.

The show, I have to admit, was not at the Birmingham Hippodrome but at the old Prince of Wales in Broad Street, shortly to become one of the earliest victims of the air-raids on the City. The blitz only served to etch deeper my memories and, when I reflect on it, if anyone is to blame for my lifelong incurable addiction to the theatre, it was the little man known as everyone's playmate.

The way life worked out, I was to meet Arthur time and time again in the years that followed.

The last time was at the Hippodrome and, once again, in

panto. He was in his last years, frail physically but robust mentally. He stood on stage, stamping his walking stick loudly and told the audience, "You've heard all the jokes before – but never better." And when I asked him for his New Year resolution, he sent me round a brief note: "Simple. Not to read my obituary in the Birmingham Mail." I reckon he did, though, back in that big balloon in the sky!

Yet another early memory, moving post-war now, was the discovery of an outstanding young impressionist in an otherwise lacklustre variety bill at the old Plaza, West Bromwich. In my cocky youthfulness I predicted a great future for him. His name? Peter Sellers.

It was in the final days of twice nightly variety that I eventually became actively involved with life at the Hippodrome, lucky to catch a glimpse of, and actually interview, the big American stars. I will never forget Lena Horne, a dazzling beauty, holding out an elegant hand and saying, "My name's Horne. What's yours?"

With her on the bill was a young English comedian who was to steal the show – even from the great Lena Horne. He introduced himself to me as Max Bygraves.

The earliest shows I reviewed at the Hippodrome were twice nightly variety – that was the order of the day. I met not only the established stars of the day but also the fast-rising unknowns like Des O'Connor. A few decades later I met a very young Cameron Mackintosh who, in those days, could hardly afford half a pint of beer and a sandwich and even borrowed money for a taxi. He was later to become the most influential figure in changing the face of theatre worldwide.

Then there were great old comedians like Norman Evans, the inspiration for Les Dawson. Les later accepted my invitation to be a guest columnist for the Mail. The result was a hazy period when we spent more time with G & T's than we did crossing the T's and dotting the I's!

Des O'Connor was the obligatory comedian touring with Buddy Holly who, while he is now one of the great Rock icons, was not doing very good business. "I taught him a few jokes and he began to get more laughs than I did", Des recalled.

Ernie Wise I still see in the 1967 *Sleeping Beauty* pantomime, going on bended knees to me to take him backstage at the Birmingham Town Hall to meet his "greatest idol" – the American bandleader Woody Herman. Even the biggest stars have their own stars!

The very first show I reviewed featured an American star, Peggy Ryan. I hated it, said so, and was duly criticised myself. Times haven't changed!

The most memorable and certainly the most important show for me was the 1964 Tony Britton *My Fair Lady*. The show set a box office record, which will probably never be broken, when it ran for a straight six months with the public still calling for more. Looking back over the broad canvas of the Hippodrome's history, I see it as the crucial, pivotal show which saved the theatre and changed the course of its destiny. It proved that the Hippodrome could not only stage big musicals but also had the audience for them.

As I look back now, names flooding my memory, colliding in my head, I reflect on how the Hippodrome has changed over the years – years that I have been fortunate, for half of the theatre's lifespan at least, to share.

In 1899, Queen Victoria was still on the throne and the country was embroiled in the costly and near-defeating second Boer War when, in the midst of the smoke-grimed Victorian buildings in Birmingham's City centre, there arose a strange tower that seemed to have taken a magic carpet ride and landed in Hurst Street straight out of the Arabian Nights. Piercing the skyline and visible from many aspects of the City centre stood a tall, slender Minaret-like tower that was to become a famous and familiar landmark in Birmingham for more than half a century - 60 years in fact. And for generations of theatregoers that distinctive tower was the symbol and trademark of the Birmingham Hippodrome.

***My Fair Lady* with Tony Britton (2nd left) as Professor Higgins, Howard Davies, Jill Martin and Gwynne Whitby in the 1964 production.**

The Moorish tower being dismantled in 1960.

Not that the building which first opened its Hurst Street doors on October 9th 1899 was then known by that name. Indeed it was not a theatre: it was a circus. Built by the Draysey brothers, James and Henry, Birmingham-born but of Bavarian descent, it was originally called the Tower of Varieties – hence that tower which remained until it was found to be unsafe in 1960 and demolished. The original auditorium seated 3,000 and there was a gallery which ran round three sides of the circus ring. There was also a proscenium stage and the hope, clearly, was that in the days to come the theatre would present both circus and music-hall.

To put no finer point on it, the place was a flop. It never saw out the year and closed within five weeks because of lack of support.

The odd thing is circus lived on in the years to come when the Royal Italian Circus arrived in style in 1925. In 1935 John Sanger's World Famous Circus visited and, believe it or not, there was even once a self-styled circus revue.

But back to the old building ... Come the new century and, under new management but still under the guidance of the original architect F.W. Lloyd, it was reconstructed, the name changed to The Tivoli and the audience capacity cut to 1,900. The builders were still hard at it when it reopened on August 20, 1900, with a variety bill with prices ranging from fourpence (less than 2p) to two shillings (10p) for a box.

It was in 1903 that it became the Birmingham Hippodrome. The dawning years of the century were reasonably successful, but it closed again in 1910, reopening with a show that featured the great Fred Karno, of Charlie Chaplin fame.

Re-enter the Draysey family in 1914 who again took over the theatre which closed yet again in 1919 before yet another rebuilding programme.

But the Hippodrome was making its mark and among the stars who appeared in those early years were Marie Lloyd, George Robey, Vesta Victoria, Dorothy Ward, Shaun Glenville, Letty Lind and Gertie Gitana.

But troubled times were ahead and it was a bit of a jolt when the theatre was put up for auction but withdrawn because the highest bid fell short by £8,000. The major provincial theatre owners, Moss Empires, bought it in 1924 and spent nearly £40,000 on improvements. The Hippodrome reopened the following year with the legendary Clarkson Rose heading the bill in a revue called *Happy Hours* and the theatre took on the appearance that remained with it throughout the next 40 years.

There seemed to be a permanence about it and its famous Minaret was as much a landmark and City symbol as the Bull Ring's Rotunda was to become. Dramatic changes began in the challenging and, for theatres, not-so-swinging Sixties.

It was after Anthony Newley finished the run of his own musical, *Stop The World – I Want To Get Off*, in June 1963, that the frontage was radically altered. No longer did it look like the entrance to a London tube station and a lavish new foyer was created.

There was also a new box office and the first Stalls bar was added to the theatre's facilities. In 1963 there was also another change of name, shortlived though it was, when the Hippodrome became the Birmingham Theatre. This led to confusion and to instances when scenery was delivered mistakenly to the Birmingham Repertory Theatre.

Moss Empires began talking about closure in 1968 but changed their minds two years later. During that period there had even been talk of converting the Hippodrome into the new Birmingham Rep.

It was in 1979 that the Hippodrome so loved and known today began to emerge. The first vital steps were taken when, in that year, Birmingham City Council purchased the theatre for £50,000. The City in turn leased the building to the Birmingham Hippodrome Theatre Trust Ltd, a non-profit making charitable organisation which took over the awesome responsibilities of both running and developing the theatre.

The original Trust membership was: David Justham, a

leading Midlands industrialist and passionate opera lover, as Chairman; Francis Graves, a prominent surveyor who played a major role in the building of the National Exhibition Centre; Len Matthews, senior resident director of the then ATV who held the franchise for the Midlands before Central; Tim Morris, Managing Director of The Birmingham Post and Mail; and two leading civic figures, Neville Bosworth and Clive Wilkinson. The Trust, which has remained small in number, is now chaired by Chris Kirk.

The success of the Hippodrome Trust has been unquestionably enhanced by its sister Development Trust, a charity solely responsible for ensuring the building fabric of the Hippodrome. Originally chaired by John Wardle, and subsequently Bruce Tanner and Alexander Patrick. Twenty years on John Hawksley now chairs the Development Trust, who are currently raising £2½ million with 'The Vital Stage Appeal' to complete the massive £28 million Centenary Development Project.

The first Director of the Hippodrome was Henry Sherwood, followed by Richard Johnston. Peter Tod, the present Director, was appointed in 1988.

Major alterations were made throughout 1981 and the theatre reopened with a production of *Jesus Christ Superstar* – a show which made such an impact when it returned in the centenary year. The purchase of the adjacent former Wesleyan Chapel, which had become a nightclub, enabled the theatre to double the size of its stage in 1984. Great strides were now being made. The Hippodrome was rapidly becoming one of the most important regional theatres in the country and in 1990, in what was described as "the major arts coup of the decade", the Sadler's Wells Royal Ballet moved from London, made its base at the theatre and became the Birmingham Royal Ballet. Enviable and impressive new headquarters were built on an adjoining site providing the most modern rehearsal studios and facilities. Subsequently, the auditorium stalls were re-raked to offer audiences more comfort and, most importantly, much improved sightlines for appreciating the ballet – which by now was appearing on the Hippodrome's stage for ten weeks each year.

Triumph after triumph now followed with such mega hits as Tommy Steele's *Singin' in the Rain*, *42nd Street*, *Joseph and the Amazing Technicolor Dreamcoat*, *Me and My Girl*, *Blood Brothers*, *Cats*, *Les Misérables* and *The Phantom of the Opera*, all running for long and highly successful seasons.

And, quite apart from being recognised as a major opera and ballet house, the Hippodrome became the unrivalled capital of British pantomime. Each year pantomime attracts more than 150,000 patrons from three- to ninety-three-year-olds, and the 1998-99 *Cinderella* broke all financial box office records in the history of British pantomime. Yes – that's right; no other theatre, London or elsewhere, can approach it. Such is the Hippodrome's standing.

In 1998/99 the theatre had a record-breaking year all round with paid admissions totalling 596,358, an audience growth of seven percent on the previous year.

And so to the future … In May 1998 the National Lottery, through the Arts Council of England, announced a £20 million contribution to the Centenary Development Project which is due to be completed in the spring of 2001. A further £2 million grant was made by the European Regional Development Fund. Birmingham City Council has given important assistance in restructuring the lease, to ensure its future for many generations to come.

The Birmingham Hippodrome will close on January 29 2000 for what has been described as "a year's interval". A new chapter, a new beginning, a new century and a new Millennium… The Hippodrome will have undergone the greatest changes of its ever-changing previous 100 years but the story will be the same, rich in memories and draped in triumphs for generations to come. And with this book I invite you to share a remarkable story of a remarkable theatre which has made its mark in the life of a remarkable City.

FRED NORRIS was born in Handsworth and originally joined the Birmingham Post and Mail in 1944 as a "pencil sharpener and copy boy". After service in the RAF he returned to Birmingham and became, among other things, cricket and rugby correspondent. He left the City in 1952, mainly working in the West Country based at Exeter. He returned to The Mail, as it then was, in 1956 and has been the theatre correspondent ever since.

Overture and beginners please!

Curtain up on the ups and downs of the early years of the theatre – from circus to music hall, from Tower of Varieties to Tivoli and, finally, the Hippodrome

WHAT A START! The poor old Hippodrome had such a disastrous beginning. Shows can open and close in a day but you expect a theatre, and a brand-new one at that, to linger on a while.

But the Hippodrome, throughout its 100 years, has always been different and it was from the moment the curtain went up. Different but hardly flattering.

The Tower of Varieties, as it was called, which opened as a circus in Hurst Street for the first time on October 9th 1899, closed weeks later.

The original idea had been to bring a taste of the seaside, Blackpool-style, to land-locked Birmingham when James and Henry Draysey hit on the idea of building their Tower of Varieties, having Blackpool Tower Circus in mind.

Within a year of that disastrous start the theatre was quickly

Birmingham, Theatre and World events 1899–1999.

1899 **Cadbury Brothers formed as a public limited company.**
Two other theatres opened in Birmingham in the same year as the Hippodrome: Oldbury Palace and Bordesley Palace.
Boer War in Africa. Widespread predictions of doom preceded the new century.

1900 **The University of Birmingham was founded by Royal Charter.**
An outbreak of bubonic plague closed Glasgow's theatres. Two of the theatre's greats died: Sir Arthur Sullivan and Oscar Wilde.
Paris hosted the World Exhibition and, later, the Olympic Games.

1901 **Marble statue of Queen Victoria unveiled in New Street (now Victoria Square).**
Richard D'Oyly Carte died.
Death of Queen Victoria. Marconi transmitted first wireless message across the Atlantic.

1902 **First Test Match at Edgbaston ground: England versus Australia.**
J.M. Barrie's 'The Admiral Crichton' premièred at the Duke of York's. The Irish Players set up.

1903 **'Buffalo Bill's Wild West Show' visited Birmingham.**
Marie Curie won the Nobel Prize for Physics. Aviation pioneers Wilbur and Orville Wright made the world's first biplane flight; it lasted 97 seconds.

1904 **Elan Valley Water supply for Birmingham opened by King Edward VII. Birmingham & Midland Motor Omnibus Company (Midland Red) formed. Cadbury's first Dairy Milk chocolate bar produced.**
Britain's first revolving stage installed at the London Coliseum. First performance of 'Peter Pan' at the Duke of York's Theatre. Royal Court seasons established Shaw's reputation as the major dramatist of the day. Miss Annie Horniman bought, converted, and subsidised a building which became the Abbey, Dublin.

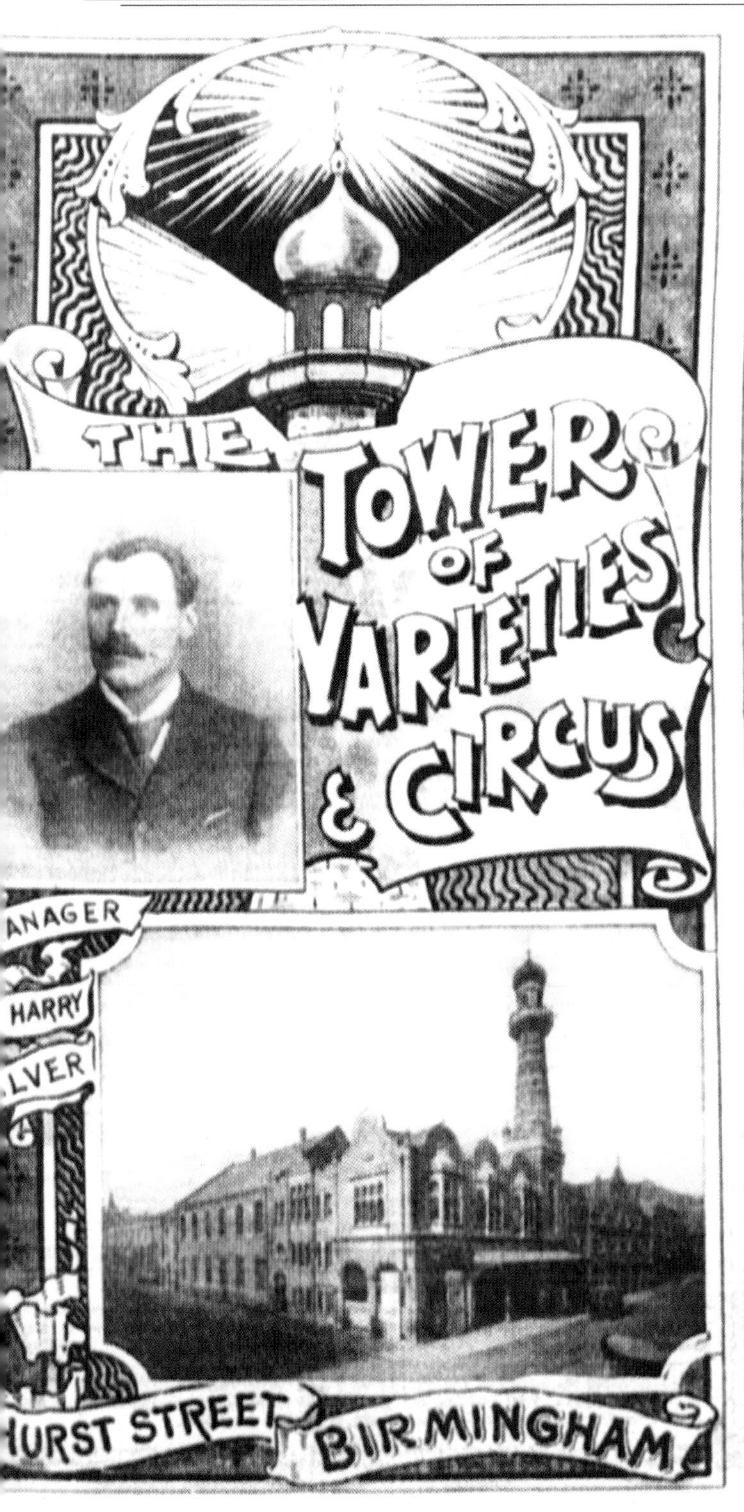

1905 **Longbridge factory set up by Herbert Austin. Birmingham became a diocese and appointed its first Bishop.**
Death of Sir Henry Irving, whilst on tour in Bradford, the first actor to be knighted. Actors in the New York production of Bernard Shaw's play, 'Mrs Warren's Profession', were prosecuted for indecency.
Russian Revolution forced the Tsar to create the Duma.

1906 **Birmingham City Football Club moved to St Andrew's. Last horse-drawn tram (in Nechells).**
Earthquake devastated San Francisco. Sir Frederick Hopkins discovered what were later to be renamed vitamins.

1907 **The first electric trams ran in Birmingham.**
Month-long strike by Music-hall artistes closed theatres all over the country. Marie Lloyd, on the picket lines, was heard to call "blacklegs!" at a troupe of performing elephants. Riots greeted the première of J M Synge's 'Playboy of the Western World'. Miss Horniman set up the first permanent repertory company in Manchester. Barry Jackson set up the Pilgrim Players in Birmingham.

1908 **First roller-skating rink in Birmingham was opened in Monument Road.**
W. Somerset Maugham had four plays running simultaneously in London.

1909 **Main University of Birmingham buildings opened by King Edward VII.**
A sensational new approach to ballet was unveiled with the inaugural season of Diaghilev's Ballets Russes in Paris, with Nijinsky and Pavlova dancing, and choreography by Fokinet. Actor Herbert Beerbohm Tree and playwright Arthur Wing Pinero were both knighted.

1910 **Electric Theatre, Station Street, opened – the first real cinema in Birmingham. Twelve months later, the city boasted seven picture houses.**
Murderer Dr Crippen was arrested aboard ship en route for Canada, the authorities having been tipped off by radio.

1911 **Last Birmingham Horse Fair held with only eleven horses and one donkey.**
The Pilgrim Players took the name of the Birmingham Repertory Company. The first performance of Chekhov's 'The

Cherry Orchard' given by the Stage Society was not well received by its audience. William S.Gilbert died. *Amundsen reached the South Pole, beating Scott by 34 days.*

1912 The first Royal Command Performance took place at the Palace Theatre. The theatrical hit of the year was 'Hullo Ragtime', an American musical at the London Hippodrome. Lilian Baylis took sole charge of the Old Vic. *The Titanic sank in the North Atlantic after hitting an iceberg.*

1913 Barry Jackson's Birmingham Repertory Theatre opened and was hailed as a major step in decentralising legitimate theatre in Britain.

1914 **Death of Joseph Chamberlain. Moor Street Station opened, replacing the temporary structure erected in 1909.**

1914-8 *Britain, France and Russia declared war on Germany following the invasion of Belgium.* Following the outbreak of war, theatres were hit by new legislation closing all bars at 9pm and banning the sale of sweets, chocolates and cigarettes after 8pm (the sale of confectionery was banned completely by 1918). The size and quality of programmes was reduced by law and each theatre was required to provide a number of men for National Service (keeping their jobs open should they return from the war). They also had to finish all performances by 10.30pm when new blackout regulations were introduced near the end of the war. Harold Brighouse's 'Hobson's Choice' had its London début. Frank Benson was knighted in the Royal Box at Drury Lane. 'Chu Chin Chow' opened at His Majesty's and ran for 2,238 performances. 'Abraham Lincoln' by John Drinkwater first performed at the Birmingham Rep.

1915 *Stonehenge sold for £6,600.*

1916 **The first attempted air-raid on Birmingham. First Municipal Savings Bank in the country opened in Birmingham.** Eden Phillpott's 'The Farmer's Wife' premièred in Birmingham. *In America, liquid nail polish was introduced – to be followed by mass*

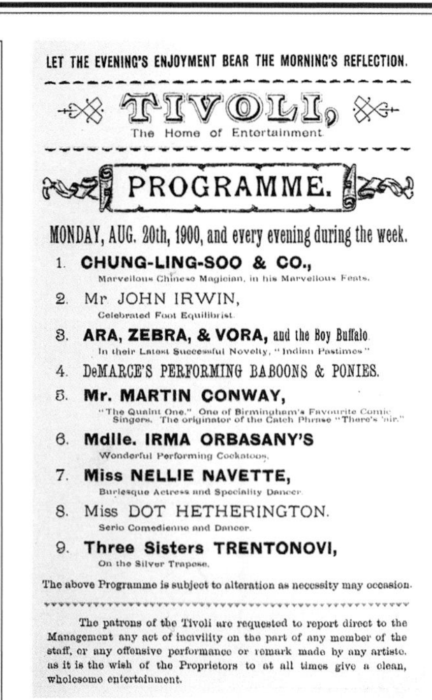

LET THE EVENING'S ENJOYMENT BEAR THE MORNING'S REFLECTION.

TIVOLI,
The Home of Entertainment

PROGRAMME.

MONDAY, AUG. 20th, 1900, and every evening during the week.

1. CHUNG-LING-SOO & CO.,
Marvellous Chinese Magician, in his Marvellous Feats.
2. Mr JOHN IRWIN,
Celebrated Foot Equilibrist.
3. ARA, ZEBRA, & VORA, and the Boy Buffalo.
In their Latest Successful Novelty, "Indian Pastimes"
4. DeMARCE'S PERFORMING BABOONS & PONIES.
5. Mr. MARTIN CONWAY,
"The Quaint One." One of Birmingham's Favourite Comic Singers. The originator of the Catch Phrase "There's 'air."
6. Mdlle. IRMA ORBASANY'S
Wonderful Performing Cockatoos.
7. Miss NELLIE NAVETTE,
Burlesque Actress and Speciality Dancer.
8. Miss DOT HETHERINGTON.
Serio Comedienne and Dancer.
9. Three Sisters TRENTONOVI,
On the Silver Trapeze.

The above Programme is subject to alteration as necessity may occasion.

The patrons of the Tivoli are requested to report direct to the Management any act of incivility on the part of any member of the staff, or any offensive performance or remark made by any artiste, as it is the wish of the Proprietors to at all times give a clean, wholesome entertainment.

The variety bill for the opening of The Tivoli in 1900.

rebuilt and given a new name: The Tivoli.

The emphasis was now on music-hall. Though they were uncertain times, the theatre was already creating milestones and it first became known as the Hippodrome in 1903.

It was the first Birmingham music-hall to present twice nightly shows. It was the first theatre to stage revue in the City. And, as the unrivalled statesman of Birmingham theatre Derek Salberg pointed out, it was the first theatre to present what later became known as the famous Crazy Shows when Fred Karno's Army catapulted on to the stage.

In these struggling times competition was intense. Showmen are traditionally reluctant to give up a fight and every

The stage, auditorium with two circles, long corridor and front entrance of the early Hippodrome

effort was made to keep the place alive, including film screenings. In the 1900s you might have seen a film at the Hippodrome like *The Curate's Day Out*, which sounds far from innocent. Newsreels were screened along with music-hall acts, which sounds like a recipe for mayhem. The newsreel of King Edward VII's coronation became part of the programme in 1902. Years later, in 1913, the theatre screened a "biggie" with *The Battle of Waterloo* closing the first half. But Dame Fortune was still not smiling on the new theatre: films like everything else failed to bring in the audiences. At one stage the theatre even experimented with a "disco" show of its day – a demonstration of gramophone records. That didn't work either. Just *what* did the public want?

It was very much a case of here today and gone tomorrow. The Hippodrome closed and opened again in 1910, was closed again in 1914 (on the outbreak of the First World War) until 1917 when it started screening films, only to close again in 1919, despite attracting the famous names of the days. Hardly a

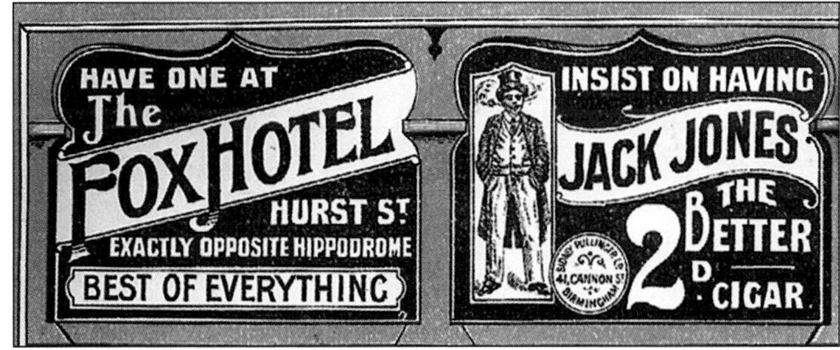

produced bright red lipstick. Conscription introduced for all men aged between 18 and 41. The Easter Rising in Ireland. Clocks went back for the first ever introduction of Summer Time.

1917 *America entered the war. Revolution in Russia.*

1918 **Eldred Hallas was elected as the first Labour MP for Birmingham.**
'Flu epidemic killed millions worldwide. The Armistice was signed, bringing the war to an end. Women given the vote for the first time in the UK.

1919 **Lickey Hills was donated to the City by the Cadbury family.**
Ellen Terry made her last major appearance as the Nurse in 'Romeo and Juliet'.
Nancy Astor was elected Britain's first woman MP.

1920 **First traffic islands erected (as a temporary measure, it was said). First concert by the City of Birmingham Orchestra at the Town Hall was conducted by Elgar.**
Cinema age launched in Hollywood.

1921 Somerset Maugham's 'The Circle' was booed at its première at the Theatre Royal Haymarket.

1922 **Launch of the four-seater Austin Seven made Austin the world leader in the light car market.**
Tutankhamen's tomb was discovered. The Morris Oxford introduced the family car in Britain.

1923 The inauguration of broadcasting by the BBC was seen by many theatres as a threat to their business, and many companies and artists refused to perform with the new medium. Oxford Playhouse opened with 'Heartbreak House', the cast included a young Flora Robson and Tyrone Guthrie. Shaw's 'Back to Methuselah' staged at Birmingham Rep - Shaw asked Jackson: " Is your family provided for?" such was the risk.
Civil War in Ireland. Hyperinflation in Germany.

1924 **First covered-top double-decker bus ran on the streets of Birmingham.**
Barry Jackson knighted for his services to theatre. Sean O'Casey's ' Juno and the Paycock' first produced at the Abbey, Dublin. 'The Vortex' by Noël Coward

first performed in London. Gershwin had his first major success on Broadway with 'Lady Be Good'.
Stalin became Russian leader following the death of Lenin.

1925 **British Industries Fair, Castle Bromwich. Birmingham's Hall of Memory was officially dedicated by Prince Arthur of Connaught.**
Hit of the year was Ben Travers' 'A Cuckoo in the Nest' at the Aldwych Theatre – the first of his farces. Drury Lane began its line of American musical spectaculars. Noël Coward's 'Fallen Angels' opened. Arnold Ridley's 'The Ghost Train' and Patrick Hamilton's 'Rope' started a trend of thrillers which was to continue.
The BBC announced that radio could reach an audience of 10 million.

1926 Peggy Ashcroft made her professional début as Margaret in 'Dear Brutus' by J.M.Barrie at the Birmingham Rep. The original Memorial Theatre in Stratford-Upon-Avon burned to the ground.
General Strike in the UK. Scottish inventor John Logie Baird projected the first television images.

1927 **The Birmingham end of the new Wolverhampton to Birmingham road opened.**
'The Desert Song' opened at the Theatre Royal Drury Lane.

1928 Ellen Terry died. In London, Jerome Kern's 'Show Boat' was the biggest musical hit for years. Lilian Baylis engaged Ninette de Valois as Ballet Mistress at the Old Vic. Walt Disney gave Mickey Mouse his début.
Alexander Fleming discovered Penicillin.

1929 **Hams Hall Power Station opened.**
Following in the footsteps of 'The Jazz Singer', the age of 'the talkies' began, with many new films using sound. Over the next few years, many of Britain's theatres were converted to cinemas as the public showed its fascination with the new medium. Barry Jackson founded the Malvern Festival which continued as an annual event for the next twelve years.
Wall Street Crash rocked the world's economy.

propitious start.

Not for the first time nor, unfortunately, for the last, the theatre seemed doomed. In the event it did not reopen until 1925, after further restyling. Now owned by Moss Empires it embarked on a new lease of life. The one-time circus blossomed as Birmingham's leading variety theatre. Already an army of famous names had stepped out on its stage:

William Claude Dukinfield, better known to the world as the irascible W.C. Fields, was so popular he made a second visit;

George Robey, one of the giants of British comedy and a vigorous defender of "good honest vulgarity";

Sir Frank Benson, proving that even in those early days when the sawdust still lingered, serious drama could grace the boards of the Hippodrome.

The opposition was certainly tough – and plentiful in the merry-go-round of Birmingham's theatre life. It had been a hard childhood, but the theatre was growing up. A brand-new chapter was opening ....

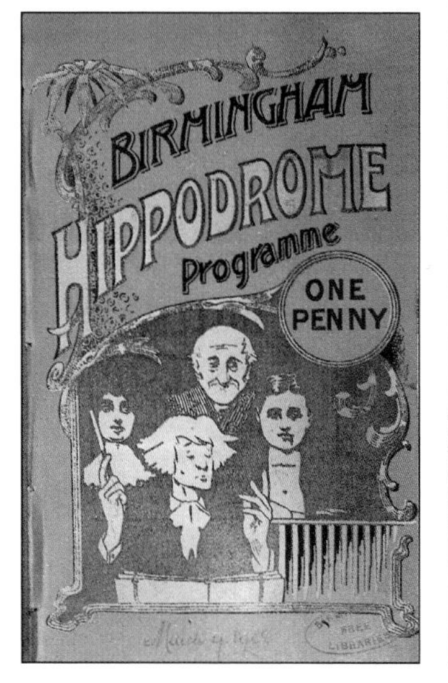

BIRMINGHAM HIPPODROME

Hurst Street, Birmingham.

Tel. No. 219 Midland. Tel. No. 219 Midland.

Proprietors: THE NEW HIPPODROME BIRMINGHAM, Ltd.
Manager: Mr. BEN DE FRECE Resident Manager & Licensee: Mr. HARRY HAMILTON

All Communications to be addressed direct to Head Office, Randwell House, 39, Charing Cross Road, London, W.C.

6-50—TWO PERFORMANCES NIGHTLY—9
On Mondays Saturdays and Holidays the First Performance will commence at 6-40

MONDAY, DEC. 16, 1912, & during the week

SCENES FROM WILD AUSTRALIA

DANCING MIDDIES
Two Neat Little Exponents of Hard Shoe Dancing

JULIAN MACK
The Dame in Topical Talk

FUN IN THE STOCKYARD

These Men and Women are not Professional Performers, but are the real rough Bush Men and Women from the Cattle Plains of the wildest parts of Australia. The men are expert manipulators of the Stock Whips and the Lasso, while the girls handle AUSTRALIAN SNAKES and CROCODILES as though they were pet dogs. See "BONITA" the most Marvellous Shot in the World. See the riding of Refractory Horses and Bucking Ponies, and Mules, some of which the public are invited to ride. A Silver Medal will be given at each performance to the Boy that rides "BUMPER," the smallest Buck Jumper in the world, and £1 will be offered to anyone who can stop ONE MINUTE ON "COOE," the Equine Whirlwind. BILLY JONAS, the Champion Rider of Buck Jumpers will undertake to ride any horse in the world.

3 LAURELS 3
In their Original Acrobatic Speciality

J. F. KEMPTON
The Johnny from St. Johns Wood, in his latest success entitled 'A Day with the Rabbits.'

DORRIMA TRIO
In Vocal Selections

HIPPODROME PICTURES
Shown on the Bioscope

AMERICA'S GREATEST AND MOST VERSATILE PERFORMER

CHAS. T. ALDRICH

THE MAN OF MANY PARTS

ALDRICH THE PROTEAN MARVEL.

ALDRICH THE TRAMP JUGGLER.

ALDRICH AS "WUN LUNG FOO."

THE GREAT AND VERSATILE ALDRICH.

The Hippodrome Grand Orchestra under the direction of Mr. T. WRATHMALL.

BOXES (5 Persons) Reserved	STALLS	CIRCLE	PIT	GALLERY
 10/6	 1/-	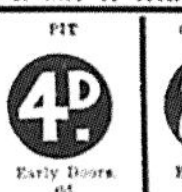 6D.	 4D.	2D.
Single Seats 2/- Booked in Advance 2/6	Early Doors 1/3 Booked 1/6	Early Doors 9d Booked 1/-	Early Doors 6d	Early Doors 3d

1ST PERFORMANCE COMMENCE 6-50. — 2ND PERFORMANCE COMMENCE 9 O'CLOCK.

Seats may be Booked by Post or Telephone 219 Midland. Box Office open 10 a.m. to 3 p.m. Seats not Guaranteed unless Booked in Advance. No Money Returned. The Management reserve the Right to Refuse Admission.

This Song must not be Sung in Music Halls and Theatres without permission

AN OLD MAN'S DARLING.

Written and Composed by FRED MURRAY and GEORGE EVERARD.

CHORUS
Some girls when they think of marriage get about all the...
Some girls when they think of marriage fancy a nice young...
But I'm not so inclined for none of those things I crave...
I'd rather be an old man's darling than a young man's slave.

SUNG BY
MISS VESTA VICTORIA.

HORWOOD & CREW LTD

BIRMINGHAM HIPPODROME

Hurst Street, Birmingham.

WHERE EVERYBODY GOES

Proprietors: THE NEW HIPPODROME BIRMINGHAM, Ltd.
Manager: Mr. BEN DE FRECE Resident Manager & Licensee: Mr. HARRY HAMILTON

All Communications to be addressed direct to Head Office, Randwell House, 39, Charing Cross Road, London, W.C.

MONDAY, AUG. 25, 1913, & during the week

W. C. FIELDS
The Silent Humorist and Originator of Everything he does.

FRED BARNES
The Birmingham Idol.

JAS. GODDEN
Comedian

THE FOUR CURTIS
In their classic and correct Step Dance Act

DEANE TRIBUNE and M'DLLE Estelle GERRERD
In Comedy Melange "A GAY DECEIVER"

JESSIE BERG
The Russian Girl with the Fiddle

DORIS TREVELYAN
The Girl with a Voice.

HIPPODROME PICTURES
Shown on the Bioscope

MR. FRANK WILSON
And COMPANY, including the Phenomenal Child Artiste

LITTLE LORNA REYARD
The Cleverest and Prettiest Little Actress in England, presents a Musical Comedietta entitled
'THE END OF THE SEASON'
By MARGARET PARKER. Incidental Music by MARK STRONG. Scenery by DRURY.

"THE BATTLE OF WATERLOO"
APPEARS HERE SHORTLY.

The Hippodrome Grand Orchestra under the direction of Mr. T. WRATHMALL.

BOXES (5 Persons) Reserved	STALLS	CIRCLE	PIT	GALLERY
 10/6	 1/-	  6D.	4D.	 2D.
Single Seats 2/- Booked in Advance 2/6	Early Doors 1/3 Booked 1/6	Early Doors 9d Booked 1/-	Early Doors 6d	Early Doors 3d

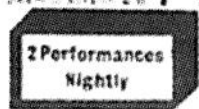

2 Performances Nightly

1st Performance starts at 6-40.
2nd Performance starts at 9 p.m.

Seats not Guaranteed unless Booked in Advance. No Money Returned. Box Office open 10 a.m. to 3 p.m. The Management reserve the Right to Refuse Admission.

The Turbulent Thirties

A decade of big bands and big names at the Hippodrome while the world veers towards another world war

THE GREAT DEPRESSION. The lure of the cinema and the growing popularity of radio. As ever, things were changing. But these were the Golden Years of light entertainment and as Birmingham's home of variety the Hippodrome came into its own.

Tom Arnold set the spectacular pattern when he introduced his first ice show, a Christmas feast which lured the audience away to a winter wonderland in Switzerland. The year was 1934.

From America came the Jazz Giants, Duke Ellington and the inimitable Thomas "Fats" Waller among them.

Ballroom dancing was at its peak – and yes, the Hippodrome led the way there too with the adjacent Tony's Ballroom the space of which was, decades later, to become an integral part of the Hippodrome. And dancing, naturally enough, brought the popularity on stage of dance bands, swiftly to become show bands and variety top-liners.

Big bands meant big names on stage at the Hippodrome including: Jack Payne, Jack Hylton (later to become an impresario), Geraldo, Billy Cotton, Henry Hall, Roy Fox, Debroy Summers, Carroll Gibbons, Nat Gonella and Mantovani – who, incidentally, began his distinguished career leading a quartet for the princely sum of £11-a-week at the old Midland Hotel (now the Burlington Hotel). When he worked at the hotel he bought his first bike; at the Hippodrome he arrived in a Rolls Royce.

George Formby was the country's top comedian, Gracie Fields the top singer. Both triumphed at the Hippodrome.

1930	**First Odeon cinema opened by Oscar Deutsch at Perry Barr.** Noël Coward starred with Gertrude Lawrence in 'Private Lives'. Jazz became the 'new wave'. Radio Luxembourg began broadcasting. Cinemas in the UK were allowed to open on Sundays, whilst theatres remained closed. *The photoflash bulb was invented. The first football World Cup was held in Uruguay. Amy Johnson made a solo flight from Britain to Australia.*
1931	**A tornado damaged property in the Small Heath area.** Lilian Baylis opened Sadler's Wells Theatre. Noël Coward's 'Cavalcade' opened. *The first trans-African railway was completed. National Government elected with Neville Chamberlain as Chancellor of the Exchequer.*
1932	The new Shakespeare Memorial Theatre opened at Stratford. John Galsworthy was awarded the Nobel Prize for Literature. 'Of Thee I Sing' was the first musical to win a Pulitzer Prize. London Philarmonic Orchestra formed by Thomas Beecham. *The Methodist Church of Great Britain and Ireland was formed.*
1933	**The city's first one-way traffic system came into operation.** Walter Greenwood's 'Love on the Dole' brought a dose of Manchester realism to London. The Open Air Theatre opened in Regents' Park. Duke Ellington's orchestra made its British début. *Hitler became German Chancellor as the Nazi Party swept to power. Violent anti-Semitism in Germany.*
1934	**The City set up a Committee to co-ordinate the building of an airport.** John Christie founded the Glyndebourne Opera Festival at his country house. *The Post Office announced the introduction of numbered postal districts to speed up deliveries.*
1935	**Neville Chamberlain became Prime Minister.** In a bid to help theatres survive in the worsening economic climate, the government agreed to a reduction in Entertainment Tax. Allen Lane started Penguin paperback books.

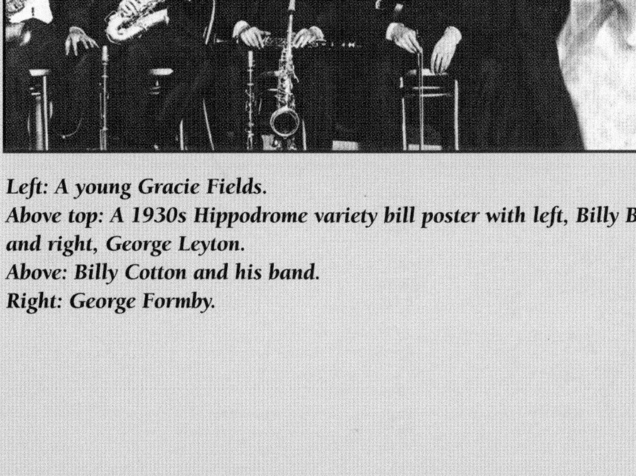

Left: A young Gracie Fields.
Above top: A 1930s Hippodrome variety bill poster with left, Billy Bennett and right, George Leyton.
Above: Billy Cotton and his band.
Right: George Formby.

1936 **A new coat of arms was granted to the City.**
The BBC started the world's first high-definition television service from Crystal Palace, London.
Controversial Olympic Games in Berlin.
Jarrow jobless marched on London.
Abdication of Edward VIII so that he could marry the American divorcee, Wallis Simpson.

1937 **Paramount Theatre opened, later to become the Odeon. The second HMS Birmingham completed (the first one had been destroyed during World War One).**
Two women who changed the face of British theatre died: Annie Horniman and Lilian Baylis. Laurence Olivier made his début at the Old Vic. Author of 'Peter Pan' Sir J.M.Barrie died.
Civil War broke out in Spain.

1938 **The foundation stone for the New Civic Centre was laid. Pageant of Birmingham in Aston Park to mark the incorporation of the borough.**
Chaos in Europe as Hitler invaded Czechoslovakia and in Asia as Japan bombed China.

1939 *Following Germany's invasion of Poland, Britain and France declared war on the Third Reich.*
Queen Elizabeth Hospital opened by King George VI and Queen Elizabeth. Birmingham Airport opened but was subsequently taken over as part of the war effort by the RAF. Over 70,000 Birmingham schoolchildren were evacuated on the outbreak of war.
Following the declaration of War on 3rd September, the government ordered the immediate closure of all theatres. However, theatres began to reopen and by Christmas most places of entertainment outside London were operational again. W.B.Yeats died. T.S. Eliot's 'Old Possum's Book of Practical Cats' was published. Council for the Encouragement of Music and the Arts and Entertainments National Service Association were formed.
World Fair in New York.

Grand, popular old names including Elsie and Doris Waters and Flotsam and Jetsam were splashed on the billboards. Broadway was represented by the irrepressible Tallulah Bankhead.

As ever, the Hippodrome was a happy spawning ground for comedy. Robb – "The Day War Broke Out" – Wilton had been a regular in his earlier days. Now he was the tops.

Sid Field was standing in the wings, waiting for his big break and in the Hippodrome's audience sat a young man from Nuneaton, Larry Grayson. Also in the audience was a 16-year-old from Hall Green who had just had his ambitions to be a sports journalist in Birmingham frustrated; now he was thinking about a career in showbiz. His name: Tony Hancock.

And Morecambe and Wise were just two kids who, while on a train one night between Birmingham and Coventry, decided to form a double act. Their names were to loom large in the Hippodrome of the future, and ultimately to become one of the icons of British entertainment in the twentieth century.

EXIT

1940 **August, first air-raid on the City over Erdington. November, highest casualties of the war: 1,353 people killed in a raid by 350 bombers. December, the Empire Theatre on the corner of Hurst Street and Smallbrook was bombed. Birmingham born statesman, Neville Chamberlain, 40th British Prime Minister, died.**
The Blitz began. Theatres in London, Birmingham, Manchester, Sheffield and other towns were destroyed or badly damaged. The raids continued for nine months.
Churchill took over as Prime Minister. Denmark, Norway, Belgium, Holland and France were invaded. Blitz on London and other British cities. British women received their pension at the age of 60.

1941 Noël Coward's 'Blithe Spirit' began a run which was to last four years.
Blitz worsened. Germany invaded Russia which then joined Britain in the war against Hitler. Japanese bombing of Pearl Harbor finally brought the U.S. into the war.

1942 Electricity rationing, shortages of all sorts of materials, manpower and other wartime measures made it increasingly difficult for Britain's theatres to stay open. Irving Berlin's 'This is the Army' hit the stage.

1943 Joseph Kesselring's 'Arsenic and Old Lace' made it into the history books as the UK's longest running play when it passed the two year mark! Oscar Hammerstein II staged the all-black 'Carmen Jones'.
Italy surrendered, war began to turn.

1944 Renewed blitz closed all but eight theatres in the West End. Joan Littlewood's Theatre Workshop was formed.
D Day landings as Allied troops moved into France. Hitler deployed V1 rockets for the first time, bringing renewed terror to British cities. The Rover Car Company introduced the Land Rover.

1945 'Peter Grimes' composed by Benjamin Britten.
Germay surrendered. First atomic bomb dropped on Hiroshima, forcing Japan to surrender. First truly electric computer built at the University of Pennsylvania.

The Roaring Forties

Throughout the war and into peacetime the top stars of stage and screen continue to entertain the Hippodrome audiences

Wilson, Keppel & Betty

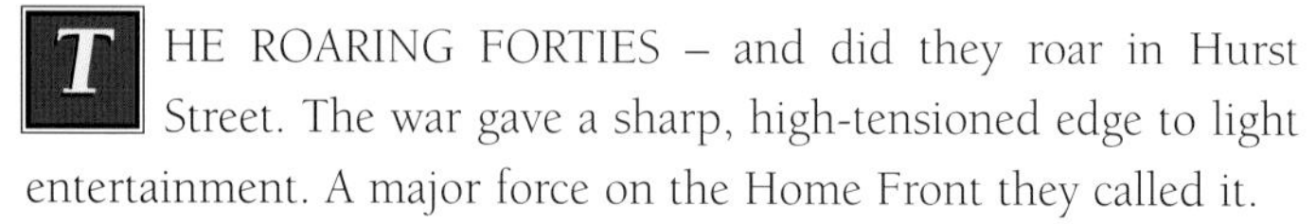

THE ROARING FORTIES – and did they roar in Hurst Street. The war gave a sharp, high-tensioned edge to light entertainment. A major force on the Home Front they called it.

And the Hippodrome, now in its element, led the way with shows as diverse – and controversial – as Mickey Spillane's sex thriller *No Orchids for Miss Blandish* and the phenomenal *This is the Army*, complete with a personal appearance from the twentieth century's most prolific composer of popular songs, the American Irving Berlin.

After the rigours and restrictions of World War Two which ended in the Far East in 1945, the glamour of Hollywood and big American stars proved irresistible, although the old favourites like George Formby could still more than hold their own.

Undoubtedly the greatest sensation was the arrival of the captivating American star and film idol Danny Kaye in 1949. The box office queue snaked for more than a quarter of a mile around the theatre. Traffic was brought to a standstill. Mounted police were brought out to control the crowds – a first glimpse of the hysteria that was to come in later years.

Another memorable incident was the arrival of Laurel and Hardy in March 1947. Theatre tickets were not available in advance for the simple reason that shows were only booked a few weeks beforehand – depending on the artist's availability, often managements had no idea what might be presented in a couple of weeks time. When word got round that Laurel and Hardy had arrived there was a stampede and near riot conditions.

This is where Lew (later Lord) Grade stepped in. He was then the boss of Moss Empires and he called in to see how bookings were going. He found a theatre besieged. He calmly opened one of the box office windows, took off his jacket and in

Jimmy Jewel and Ben Warriss

Danny Kaye on stage, and with the Lord Mayor and Lady Mayoress during his visit to Birmingham in 1949.

1946 **Birmingham elected its first Labour-controlled City Council.**
Alec Guinness received rave reviews for his appearance as the Fool in 'King Lear' at the Old Vic, and Ralph Richardson was equally successful in J.B. Priestley's 'An Inspector Calls'. The Arts Council of Great Britain was created. The BBC started the Third Programme (now Radio 3).
The National Health Service was founded. Divorce rate in Britain soared as soldiers returned from the war. New austerity measures were introduced in the face of economic crisis in the UK, with even tighter rationing of clothing, food, petrol and currency. Juan Peron elected as president of Argentina.

1947 **The heaviest snowfall on record in Birmingham.**
During the coldest winter in living memory, audiences struggled through snowdrifts to get to productions, often only to find that power-cuts had blacked out the performances. Hits of the year in London were 'Annie Get Your Gun' and 'Oklahoma!'
The first Edinburgh International Fesival opened.
India and Pakistan became independent within the British Commonwealth. Britain's coal industry was nationalised.

1948 **Birmingham replaced Glasgow as Britain's "second city" with a population of 1,096,000.**
Inauguration of the National Health Service, together with National Insurance and Unemployment Benefit. The "Austerity" Olympics in London. First supersonic flight by a US plane. Railways, the electricity industry and gas were all nationalised. Bread rationing came to an end. The World Health Organisation was founded. The first long-playing record was released by Columbia Record Company.

1949 **Television came to Birmingham with the inauguration of the BBC's Sutton Coldfield transmitter.**
Rodgers and Hammerstein's 'South Pacific' first produced.
In South Africa 'apartheid' came into being. First atomic bomb test in the USSR.

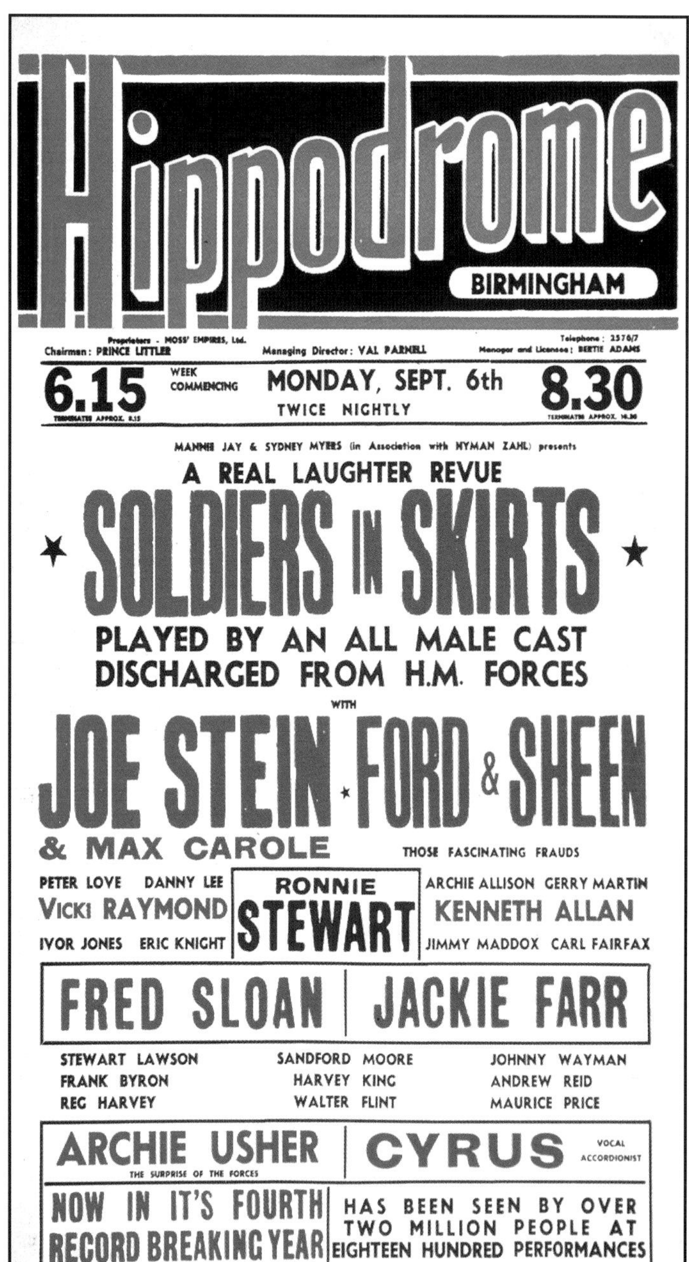

waist-coated shirt-sleeves opened up for trade. It is said, perhaps tongue-in-cheek, that he broke a record for handling cash-over-the-counter sales. But that's one we shall never really know!

Twice nightly was very much alive but a whole world was opening up and the Hippodrome was swift to embrace it – and the remarkable range of the theatre's offerings came sharply into focus.

On the one hand the Hippodrome stage supported the plumed struttings of the long-legged beauties from the famous Folies Bergères in Paris, on the other, classical music concerts. One conductor, an American comedian who was later to become Winston Churchill's son-in-law, was Vic Oliver and, on 25 April 1948, he conducted the British Concert Orchestra in a programme of Beethoven, Tchaikovsky and Grieg.

Again this was a sign of things to come. In future years the Hippodrome would become the temporary home of the City of Birmingham Symphony Orchestra for a summer prom season in 1972 when their home base, the Town Hall, was being refurbished.

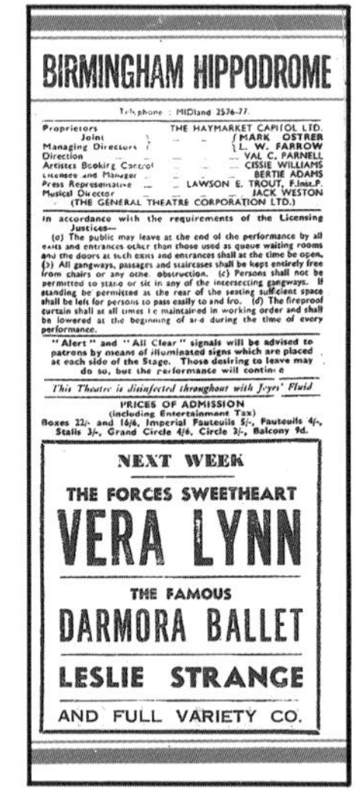

Sid Field, more famous as 'SLASHER GREEN', the Birmingham comedian and film star, hailed as the funniest clown since Charlie Chaplin.

1950 **The first hole-in-the-heart operation in England was performed at Birmingham Children's Hospital.**
The charismatic playwright Bernard Shaw died aged 94. Statistics showed that in a big city about 3% of the population could be relied on to visit the theatre weekly.
End of petrol rationing saw a boom in motoring. British troops sent to Korea. British football teams competed for the first time in the World Cup.

1951 **Birmingham twinned with the French City of Lyon.**
Two great musicals, 'Kiss Me Kate' and 'South Pacific' received their British premières. Ivor Novello died.
Festival of Britain gave a huge boost to the nation's morale.

1952 **St Patrick's Day Parade took place in Birmingham—the first English city to hold such an event.**
Agatha Christie's play 'The Mousetrap' opened at the Ambassadors Theatre. 'The Flowerpot Men' became part of BBC's programming.
Death of King George VI. The Coronation of Queen Elizabeth II.

1953 **The last tram to run in the city, No. 616, left Steelhouse Lane terminus for Erdington.**
Edmund Hillary and Tensing Norgay reached the summit of Mount Everest. Hurricanes bought devastating floods to the East Coast of England. Khrushchev took over as Russian leader following the death of Stalin. Britain celebrated the coronation of its new Queen, Elizabeth II.

1954 **Volumes 1 and 2 of J.R.R. Tolkien's 'The Lord of The Rings' were published.**
Julian Slade's 'Salad Days' opened. Dylan Thomas' 'Under Milk Wood' was broadcast on BBC's Third Programme.
The polio vaccine was released for general use. Roger Bannister was the first man to run a mile in under 4 minutes.

1955 **Colleges of Technology, Commerce and Art opened by the Queen.**
Commercial television began to broadcast.
Walt Disney spent £4.5 million on the construction of Disneyland.

The Rocking-Rolling Fifties

The arrival of the Broadway musical helps the Hippodrome survive the challenges of the small screen and the Rock 'n' Roll explosion

Patrons queuing in Inge Street for Hippodrome tickets.

TURMOIL. YEARS OF CHANGE. The arrival of commercial television. The Rock 'n' Roll explosion. The dying pangs of twice nightly variety. To many lovers of theatre this was a disastrous decade – they saw them as the days when family audiences were driven away by the Rock stampede as shrieking, uncontrollable audiences, scarcely out of their nappies, tore up seats and charged the stage like hysterical hooligans.

And yes, they were right. The Fifties were furious. They did lash theatres. But there was another side to the coin. Good things were to emerge. Tommy Steele with his peroxide-blond hair and young Cliff Richard trying to be a polite Elvis Presley began to make their mark.

Variety, with the advent of commercial television, took a mighty tumble – but don't forget this was the decade when Frank Sinatra arrived at the Hippodrome in a vital, critical stage of his remarkable career – a career that was to change the singing voice of the world when everyone started sporting pork-pie hats and loud bow-ties and amateur talent shows overflowed with Sinatra look-and-sound-alikes.

The Hippodrome's role was already changing. Variety might be on the way out but musicals were coming in.

And so it was the decade when the great post-war invasion of the Broadway musicals began to steamroll in, starting with *Annie Get Your Gun*, through to *Brigadoon* and *Carousel*. British musicals, not to be outdone, held their heads high.

Unforgettable was vivacious Cicely Courtneidge in Ivor Novello's *Gay's the Word* and delightful Anna Neagle in *The Glorious Days*. It was the decade when spectacular ice shows came into their own – a big, fast-moving and colourful answer to the challenge of the small screen at home. Often at Christmas,

1956 **Theatre Royal demolished. First multi-storey car park opened.**
Both the Bolshoi Ballet and the Berliner Ensemble made their first visits to England. 'Look Back in Anger' by John Osborne had its première at the Royal Court Theatre. This was the first outstanding success for the English Stage Company, and is now considered to be a landmark in modern theatre. American singer, Elvis Presley, dominated rock music after the release of 'Heartbreak Hotel'. Britain started The Eurovision Song Contest.
Uprising in Hungary, later suppressed by Soviet troops. Britain and France invaded Egypt after Nasser nationalised the Suez Canal. FORTRAN, the first computer language was invented.

1957 **Rackhams opened in Corporation Street.**
Laurence Olivier played Archie Rice in Osborne's 'The Entertainer' at the Royal Court and then transferred to the West End. Vivien Leigh created a stir in the House of Lords when she protested at the demolition of the historic St. James' Theatre, London. New television programmes included 'The Sky at Night' with Patrick Moore.
Treaty of Rome signed by France, West Germany, Belgium, Netherlands, Italy and Luxembourg, creating the European Common Market. Sputnik 1 launched by USSR, circling the earth for 95 minutes.

1958 Peter Shaffer's 'Five Finger Exercise' produced in London. Sybil Thorndike and Sir Lewis Casson celebrated their Golden Wedding Anniversary. Britain's first post-war municipally built repertory theatre opened - the Belgrade in Coventry.
Eight members of Manchester United Football team were killed in an air crash at Munich. The first section of British motorway was opened in December near Preston, and closed soon after because of frost damage!

1959 The Mermaid Theatre opened with 'Lock Up Your Daughters' which was an immediate success.
Birmingham-built Mini Minor cars first went on sale at £500. Britain experienced its driest summer for 200 years.

sometimes in the summer too these shows, largely presented by that great showman Tom Arnold, went a long way in the fight to bring back family audiences to the theatre.

It was also the decade when the Hippodrome launched its first pantomime – *Jack and the Beanstalk* in 1957 with Beryl Reid, Reg Dixon and a young lady who was to be very popular with the later Hippodrome audiences, Audrey Jeans.

We perhaps didn't appreciate it at the time but from that particular beanstalk grew a new tradition that the Hippodrome would make exclusively its own.

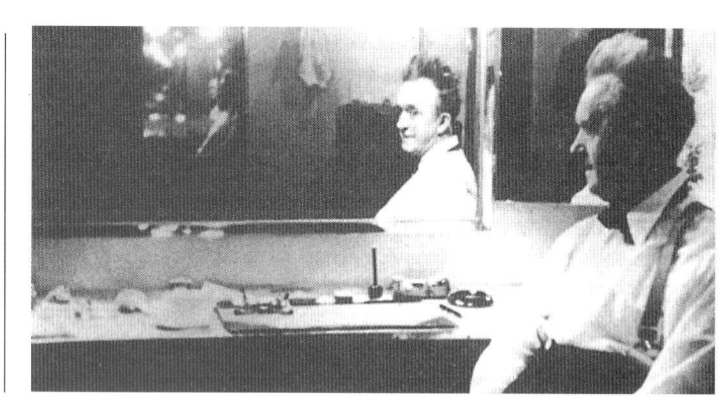

'The Dancing Years' by Ivor Novello, on ice at The Hippodrome

Rodgers and Hammerstein's original production of 'Carousel'

The Swinging Sixties

1960 **First section of the Inner Ring Road opened at Smallbrook Ringway, (now called Smallbrook Queensway).** Lionel Bart's 'Oliver!', Britain's first major homegrown musical took London by storm. The Beatles formed. Peter Hall was appointed Director of the Royal Shakespeare Company.

1961 Sir Barry Jackson died. Shakespeare Memorial Theatre renamed Royal Shakespeare Theatre and the Royal Shakespeare Company acquired a London base at the Aldwych Theatre. The Royal Court premièred 'Luther' with Albert Finney in the title role. Ballet dancer Rudolf Nureyev defected for freedom in the West. *Yuri Gagarin became the first human to go into space. He ventured 190 miles up before turning his Vostok spacecraft back earthward. The Berlin Wall was built.*

1962 It was estimated that 80% of all touring theatre productions still transported scenery and artistes by train! Chichester Festival Theatre opened under Sir Laurence Olivier's direction. 'Dr No', the first James Bond film, hit the cinemas. *Marilyn Monroe found dead. US and USSR came to the brink of war over the Cuban missile crisis.*

1963 **Birmingham City FC won the League Cup beating Aston Villa.** The National Theatre gave its first performance with Peter O'Toole in Sir Laurence Olivier's production of 'Hamlet' at the Old Vic. Littlewood's 'Oh, What a Lovely War!' opened. *The Great Train Robbery in Buckinghamshire. Martin Luther King made his "I have a dream" speech. US President Kennedy assassinated in Dallas.*

1964 **The Bull Ring Centre opened by the Duke of Edinburgh. The development included a new bus station. The new Crescent Theatre was completed, replacing the original building which opened in April 1932. Work began on the Castle Vale Estate.** The Windmill Theatre which boasted that it never closed actually closed.

1965 **The new Post and Mail building was opened by Princess Margaret. Birmingham and Midland Institute**

'In spite of the long running success of My Fair Lady the Hippodrome faces the constant and growing threat of closure'.

"Now it's My FAB Lady"

FRED NORRIS, EVENING MAIL

After appearing 'bottom-of-the-bill' in March 1963, The Beatles returned with two sell-out performances in November. In an attempt to avoid the screaming fans, the Birmingham Police disguised them with helmets to get them in and out of the Hippodrome!

BUILD THE SET SO that it can fit the stage of the Birmingham Hippodrome – then it will fit any theatre in the country. That was the order of the day sent out by Leslie A. MacDonnell, one-time agent for Vera Lynn and, at the time, managing director of Moss Empires. But it was that order of the day which underlined the theatre's peculiar plight: it had the audience for big shows but it did not have the facilities.

The show he had in mind was *My Fair Lady* which, after its original triumph in New York and London with Rex Harrison and Julie Andrews, was now about to embark on a national tour opening in Birmingham with the City's own star, Tony Britton, as Professor Higgins and Jill Martin as Eliza.

The year was 1964, the month August. It turned out to be a milestone in the history of the theatre. It ran on and on, and even spilled over into the Christmas season. It ran for six months and was so popular it was swiftly brought back for another season, this time with Wendy Bowman as Eliza, to make it one of the Hippodrome's greatest all-time attractions.

Far from drawing audiences away from the theatre, television opened new doors. One of the great hits of the decade was the stage version of television's *The Black and White Minstrel Show* which was given a triumphant try-out at the Hippodrome.

It was not without controversy. It was the first show to be mimed to allow the dancers more freedom of movement. Controversy remained when it became one of the first shows to be screened in colour by the BBC; the girls were all dressed in black and white!

But then, the same thing happened in *My Fair Lady* on stage. The famous Cecil Beaton Ascot scene was entirely in black and white.

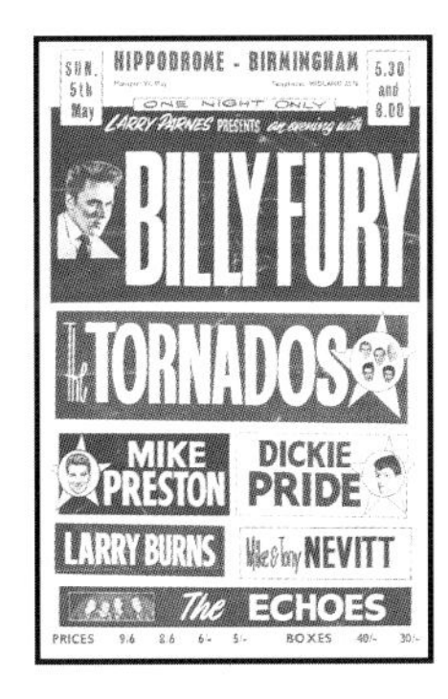

was demolished to make way for the new Central Library.
Cigarette advertising is banned from TV. The Beatles were awarded MBEs.

1966 **Tripartite agreement signed between Birmingham, Lyon and Frankfurt.**
Joe Orton's 'Loot' opened at the Royal Court Theatre.
England won the football World Cup. Carnaby Street in London became a fashion mecca.

1967 **The first West Indian policeman in Britain, PC Ralph Ramadhar, went on patrol in the city. The rebuilt New Street Station opened, as did the new Birmingham Mint in Warstone Lane. The city also got a new landmark, the 350 feet tall Post Office Tower (498 ft if you include the spire).**
Start of colour television. Meanwhile, on black and white television, 'The Forsyte Saga' caused churches to alter their service times or run the risk of the church emptying before the start of the programme. The murder of Joe Orton.
The world's first heart transplant operation took place in Cape Town.

1968 **First major road tunnel under the City opened at St Chad's Circus. Serbian Orthodox church opened in Bournville faithfully based on a 14th century Byzantine design.**
Theatre censorship in Britain ended after centuries of control from the office of the Lord Chamberlain. The following evening 'Hair' opened in London. Sadler's Wells Opera moved to the Coliseum and subsequently changed its name to English National Opera. This year saw a huge increase in the number of fringe companies formed.
"I'm Backing Britain" campaign to support British enterprise. Serious riots in France. In the US, Martin Luther King and Robert Kennedy were assassinated. Czechoslovakia's liberalising reforms were crushed when Soviet troops invaded.

1969 **Last Onion Fair held at Serpentine Fairground, Aston.**
Civil Rights demonstrations in Northern Ireland and British troops stationed there. Concorde made its inaugural flight. Neil Armstrong became the first man to walk on the moon.

Ken Dodd, The Honeys and Wilf May, manager of The Hippodrome, with Fred Norris (second left) pick the winner from the Birmingham Mail competition during the 1965–66 record breaking panto "Humpty Dumpty".

My Fair Lady continued her romance with the Hippodrome in the years to come. Liz Robertson, the sixth wife of the lyricist Alan Jay Lerner, co-starred with Tony Britton for a new Cameron Mackintosh production in 1979 and, with Denis Quilley (a former Birmingham Rep actor), for a further, lavish production in the 1980s.

Romance, though, was not in the air when the show returned to the Hippodrome, this time with a Simon Callow production in 1991. It starred Edward Fox as Higgins along with a talented newcomer, Helen Hobson as Eliza. She received the good notices. The show took a belting and provoked the headline, "No Way To Treat A Lady".

The decade also saw discussions about the Hippodrome becoming an opera house after the Sadler's Wells Opera production of *Orpheus in the Underworld* was blessed with a sensational performance by the Australian singer, June Bronhill. Business was not good. But the die had been cast... The Hippodrome could stage opera – although it was to take another eleven years before the Welsh National Opera decided to make their Midlands base at the Hippodrome, having previously appeared at the Alexandra Theatre.

The lack of consistently good productions – and the 'explosion' of television into the majority of homes in Britain – meant that threats of closure persisted and there was even a serious suggestion that the Hippodrome should become the new Birmingham Repertory Theatre.

Somehow the Hippodrome survived.

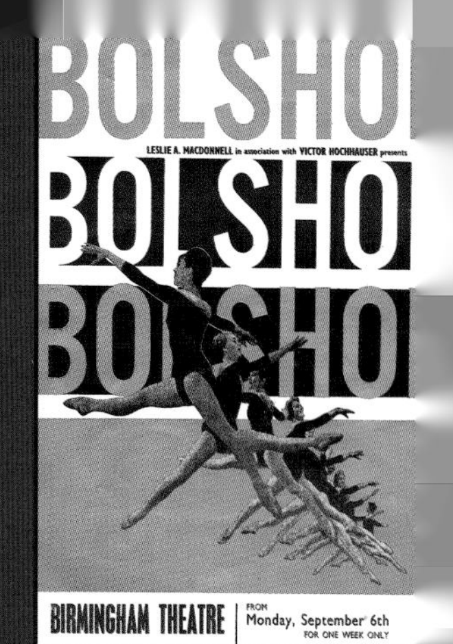

Margaret Rutherford and Sid James, two of the greatest celebrities of the stage, as they appeared together in The Solid Gold Cadillac.

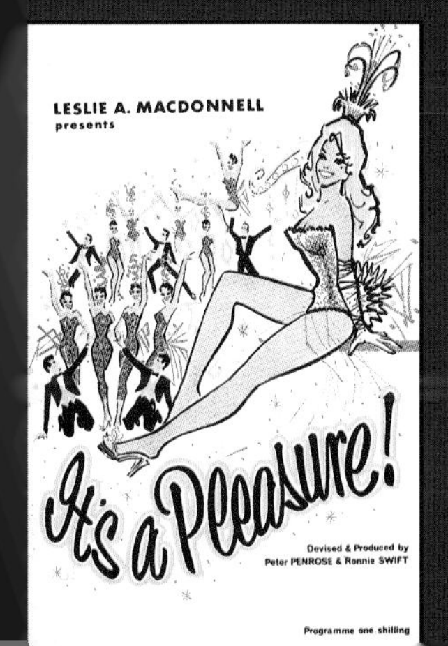

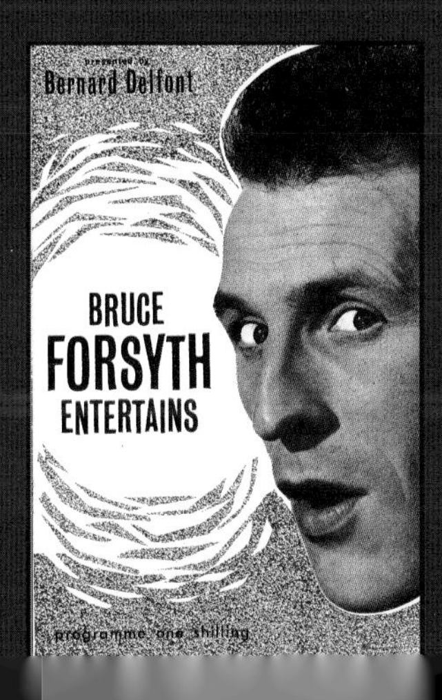

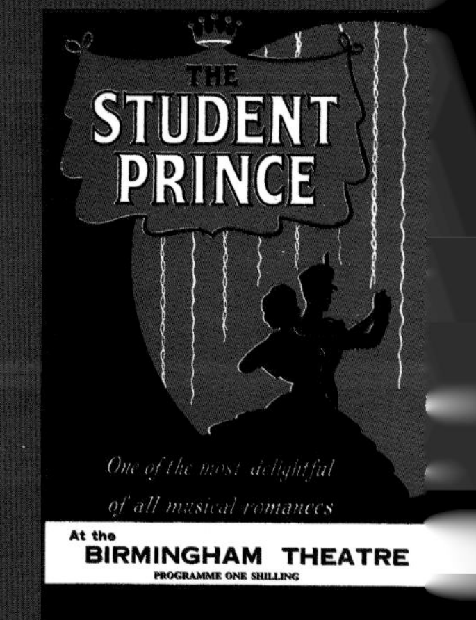

1970 **M5/M6 motorway link opened.**
A flu epidemic closed theatres all over the country. Later in the year, 'The Mousetrap' took over from 'The Drunkard' (in Los Angeles) as the world's longest-running play. 'Oh! Calcutta!' opened at the Roundhouse, London. Noël Coward was knighted. A year after it was first broadcast, 'Monty Python's Flying Circus' transferred from BBC2 to BBC1.
Bangladesh became independent from Pakistan.

1971 **The Queen opened the Inner Ringway and mistakenly named the entire route Queensway. The new Birmingham Repertory Theatre opened by HRH Princess Margaret in Broad Street.**
Peter Brook's groundbreaking production of 'A Midsummer Night's Dream' won high praise throughout the world.

1972 Pickets delayed the opening of 'Jesus Christ Superstar', claiming that it was blasphemous. The Half Moon Theatre in London and The Crucible in Sheffield were both opened.
Worsening situation in Northern Ireland. IRA bombing campaign spread to the rest of the UK.

1973 **Balsall Heath Mosque opened; the most magnificent of several in the city. The third HMS Birmingham launched.**
Première of 'The Rocky Horror Show' at the Royal Court. Sir Noël Coward died.
US and Vietnam signed a Peace Treaty in Paris, bringing to an end years of war. Revelations about the bugging of the Democratic Conference led (the following year) to the resignation of US President Nixon. Coup in Chile as Pinochet seizes power. Economic crisis brought three-day working week to the UK.

1974 **The Central Library was opened by Harold Wilson. The first cycle race on the streets of the City centre. The first ever strike by nurses in Britain took place at Erdington's Highcroft Hospital and lasted exactly 24 hours. Birmingham pub bombs exploded in two city-centre bars: the Mulberry Bush and the Tavern-in-the-Town, killing 21 and injuring many.**
Sir Peter Hall became Director of the National Theatre. Alan Ayckbourne's

The Seventies of Change

A former Rock 'n' Roll star breaks all box office records for a musical but the theatre faces continuing threats to its future

TOMMY STEELE WAS BACK. That same tousle-haired pioneer of British Rock 'n' Roll who caused near riots in the fifties was now creating record-breaking but quite orderly queues at the box office. How times change! And how, in this decade, the Hippodrome was about to change!

Meanwhile, the "Rock with the Caveman" teenager was emerging as an international star, dancing both with Fred Astaire and Gene Kelly, making a name for himself both on Broadway and in Hollywood and, of course, at the Hippodrome.

The show was *Hans Andersen*, originally created in Hollywood by Frank Loesser as a vehicle for Danny Kaye. It had taken Harold Fielding more than seven years of negotiation to secure the stage rights from Sam Goldwyn. Tommy Steele then collaborated with playwright Beverley Cross in writing a new stage book to go with Loesser's musical score. This sensational

'The Norman Conquests' opened and made a new star - Penelope Keith. The Other Place in Stratford-upon-Avon was opened.

1975 **The City's last remaining gas lamp was taken down in Duke Street, Gosta Green. Sleet and snow was recorded in June at Edgbaston Observatory for the first time ever. A new town-twinning agreement was signed with Milan.**
Sir John Gielgud and Sir Ralph Richardson joined forces in Pinter's new play 'No Man's Land'.
Britain voted to join the EEC. North Sea Oil began to flow.

1976 **The National Exhibition Centre was opened by the Queen.**
The National Theatre opened on the Southbank in London, having been in planning for more than half a century. Playgoers mourned the death of three great Dames of the theatre: Agatha Christie, Sybil Thorndike and Edith Evans. The Royal Exchange Theatre in Manchester opened.
John Curry won gold medal for skating at the Montreal Olympics.

1977 Royal Shakespeare Company opened a second studio theatre in London, The Warehouse. Elvis, Maria Callas, Bing Crosby, Terence Rattigan and Charlie Chaplin died during the year.
The Queen's Silver Jubilee celebrations. Punk rock made it onto television and into the charts.

1978 Andrew Lloyd Webber and Tim Rice's 'Evita' broke records in the West End, opening with the largest ever advance sales.
Polish Cardinal Karol Wojtyla appointed Pope John Paul II, the first non-Italian Pope since 1522.

1979 Peter Shaffer's 'Amadeus' provided a major hit for the National Theatre, with Paul Scofield as Salieri and Simon Callow as Mozart. 'Annie' was awarded the London Critics' Award for best Musical. The Lyric, Hammersmith rebuilt with a new studio theatre.
Revolution in Iran; American hostages held. Russians invaded Afghanistan. Sir Anthony Blunt, the Queen's art advisor, was revealed as the "fourth man" in the Soviet spy ring.

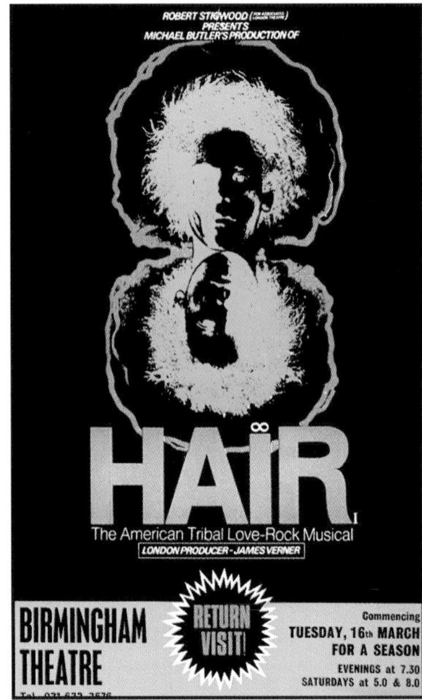

Right: 'Hello, Dolly!' with Dora Bryan

show proved to be one of the biggest successes the theatre had known and took £1.5 million in advance at the box office, more than any theatre outside London had ever achieved.

Tommy Steele's box office record went unbroken until 1994 when *Joseph and the Amazing Technicolor Dreamcoat*, starring Phillip Schofield, took an equally amazing £3.2 million in advance sales. But back to the seventies; another big hit was *Hair*, the show that lifted the veil – and other forms of clothing – from theatre censorship laws in Britain. In contrast Dora Bryan, always popular in Birmingham, scored a personal triumph in *Hello, Dolly!*

But despite all these smash hits, the menacing clouds of uncertainty still hung over the Hippodrome. Its future remained in doubt. Something, desperately, had to happen. And then, like the appearance of the Good Fairy in a Paul Elliott pantomime, it did.

There followed what will undoubtedly be recorded as the most important year in the history of the theatre. In 1979 – eighty years after it first opened its doors – the City of Birmingham, with terrific personal support from Councillors Neville Bosworth and Freda Cox, purchased the freehold for £50,000 from Moss Empires and leased it to the Birmingham Hippodrome Theatre Trust Ltd, a charitable trust managed by Birmingham people.

A refurbished theatre, within the shell of the old was about to be born. Like Tommy Steele, who had blossomed from a raucous cheeky cockney Rock 'n' Roll singer to become one of the biggest stars in the business, so the former circus and music-hall began to take its first firm, if still tiny, steps towards becoming the home of a Royal Ballet company, and one of the most prestigious centres for opera, musicals, pantomime and entertainment in the country.

And while there was a great deal to do, and a tremendous lot of money required to put things right, that tingle began to dance along the spine.

One sensed that a new star was about to be born.

'All I Want Is A Room Somewhere'. Liz Robertson as Eliza Doolittle in Cameron Mackintosh's 1979 production of 'My Fair Lady'

The Exciting Eighties

1980 **Rededication of St Philip's Cathedral to celebrate the completion of restoration work. CBSO diamond jubilee season. The Arena was added to the NEC complex, for sporting and musical events.**
Peter O'Toole's catastrophic production of 'Macbeth'. Howard Brenton's 'Romans in Britain' caused a furore. Royal Shakespeare Company's two part 'Nicholas Nickelby' was an international success. The half price theatre ticket booth opened in Leicester Square.
Sony launched the 'Walkman'.

1981 **The refurbished Hippodrome reopened with 'Jesus Christ Superstar'.**
'Cats' opened to sensational reviews at the New London Theatre. Michael Crawford opened at the Palladium in 'Barnum'.
Britain had a day off work to watch the wedding of Prince Charles and Lady Diana. The IBM company launched its personal computer. The first London Marathon was run. Riots in Birmingham, Chester, Hull, Liverpool, London, Preston, Reading and Wolverhampton, repeating the pattern of the disorder in Bristol in 1980.

1982 **Aston Villa won the European Cup, beating Bayern München 1-0: the first time ever that a West Midlands club had won the cup.**
Opening of the Barbican Centre, the new London home for the London Symphony Orchestra and the Royal Shakespeare Company. 'Guys and Dolls' opened at the National Theatre to great acclaim. Channel 4 started transmission.
UK unemployment reached record levels. Falklands war followed the invasion of the islands by Argentina. CD players went on sale.

1983 Sir Ralph Richardson died.
The wearing of seat belts by front seat passengers was made compulsory. The first US woman went into space.

1984 **Birmingham International Airport opened by the Queen.**
Highlights of the year were '42nd Street' at Drury Lane and 'Starlight Express' which had roller skating tracks built as part of the set. The Arts Council of

Now owned by the people of Birmingham, the Hippodrome enters an exciting period of change and development

THIS IS WHEN IT ALL STARTED to happen: times of rapid change.

Sadly, it meant the theatre had to close its doors on several occasions, the first time right at the beginning of the new decade. After the show *Elvis – the Musical,* in July 1980, the first major phase of a range of improvements was put in hand.

A totally refurbished theatre greeted audiences to *Jesus Christ Superstar* a year later. More than £2 million had been spent backstage and the audience sat wide-eyed in a "new", renovated auditorium, marvelling at its splendour.

Within a couple of years there was another massive burst of work, undoubtedly the most important ever because, while it may not have changed the face of the theatre, it radically altered the capabilities of the Hippodrome.

At long last it became the major lyric stage outside London

The original stage demolished for extension in 1983.

Barry Hopson (Theatre Manager), Cilla Black and Richard Johnston (Theatre Director) launch the 1983/4 panto 'Jack And The Beanstalk'.

Lulu as Miss Adelaide in 'Guys and Dolls'.

Tommy Steele in the stage production of, 'Singin' in the Rain' at the Hippodrome, after a long run at the London Palladium.

with the backstage space to house the biggest and best shows available. This was possible because of the purchase of property at the rear of the theatre.

And in the area that had formerly housed a chapel which went on to become a nightclub, the Hippodrome was able to transform its own capacities. It doubled the depth and size of the stage space.

Those nightmare days of cramped productions, highlighted by the specially designed *My Fair Lady* in the sixties, were now over.

First show in – and one that could not have been staged before – was the spectacular Andrew Lloyd Webber *Song and Dance*, starring Marti Webb and Wayne Sleep. A flush of major shows began to fill the stage; ironically one was a flashback to the Hippodrome's very first days, given by The Moscow State Circus.

Lulu, the one-time teenage pop singer, made her début with the National Theatre in the smash hit musical *Guys and Dolls*.

Great Britain report 'The Glory of the Garden' about regional arts was published.
After discoveries about the extent of acid rain damage to the UK's flora and fauna, scientists revealed that global warming could present an infinitely greater threat to the environment. After several years of research, the AIDS virus was identified. The Band Aid single, 'Do They Know It's Christmas?' raised £8 million for famine relief in Africa. Dr Alec Jeffreys of the University of Leicester discovered that a core sequence of DNA is unique to each person.

1985 **Handsworth Riots in September.**
Hit of the year was the Royal Shakespeare Company's musical adaptation of Victor Hugo's massive novel, 'Les Misérables'. Opening of the Swan Theatre in Stratford. Willy Russell had to go on as Shirley Valentine in the eponymous play when his leading lady fell ill. Ted Hughes was appointed Poet Laureate.
Mikhail Gorbachev became Soviet leader, promising an era of reform. Two years after they were introduced, CDs started to make a dent in the sale of LPs.

1986 **First Birmingham Superprix was abandoned after 26 laps due to torrential rain. International Convention Centre foundation stone was laid by Jacques Délors, President of the European Commission.**
Up and down the country, touring theatres reopened after refurbishment. Bradford Alhambra, marked one of the finest of these refurbishments to date. 'The Phantom of the Opera' opened at Her Majesty's Theatre. The Arts Council of Great Britain's Enquiry into Professional Theatre in England (The Cork Report) was published. The Swan Theatre at Stratford-upon-Avon opened.
Explosion at the Chernobyl nuclear reactor in the Ukraine sent fall-out over much of Northern Europe. The return of Haley's Comet.

1987 **Snow Hill Station re-opened. Prince Charles called the Central Library a "concrete missile silo".**
Opening of the Theatre Museum in London. Kenneth Branagh set up the Renaissance Theatre Company. First British staging of 'Porgy and Bess'.
Work began on the Channel Tunnel. 110-mile-an-hour winds brought unprecedented destruction to parts of southern and eastern England, causing more than £300 million worth of damage. "Black Monday" saw a huge fall in share prices and wiped 10 percent off the value of the stock market. There was a formal announcement that the world's population stood at 5,000,000,000 – double the level in 1950.

1988 **The CBSO made a live satellite broadcast simultaneously to the US and the UK from a concert in Los Angeles.**
'Miss Saigon' opened at the Theatre Royal Drury Lane. Sir Peter Hall left the National Theatre and Richard Eyre was appointed Director. Maureen Lipman triumphed in her one-woman show 'Re:Joyce'. At the age of 84 Sir John Gielgud performed in 'The Best of Friends'.
A year of transport tragedies in the UK. A train-crash at Clapham was quickly followed by two air disasters: a Pan Am jumbo jet ploughed into the Borders town of Lockerbie after a bomb exploded on board, later a Belfast-bound flight from Heathrow crash-landed on the M1 motorway.

1989 **Paradise Circus was lowered, allowing pedestrians direct access to Centenary Square from Chamberlain Square.**
Sir Anthony Quayle and Lord Olivier died. Shakespeare's Rose Theatre was rediscovered alongside the Globe. Lloyd Webber's 'Aspects of Love' first performed at the Prince of Wales Theatre.
Launch of satellite television. Pro-democracy demonstrations were quashed in Beijing. All over Eastern Europe, there was sweeping political change as the Communist era came to a bloodless end. In Berlin, the wall was breached and then dismantled.

The first two Chairmen of the Birmingham Hippodrome Theatre Trust, David Justham (left) who was succeeded by Tim Morris (right).

Actor and impresario Paul Elliott, an early *Dixon of Dock Green* television star, made his début as the Hippodrome pantomime producer with Russ Abbot giving him instant success.

Hollywood stars and the occasional straight play still beckoned and one of the most distinguished American leading ladies to arrive was Lauren Bacall in the Tennessee Williams' powerful drama *Sweet Bird of Youth*, prior to its London opening.

And, of course, there was the spectacular 1987 visit by the Kirov Opera.

In 1986 the theatre underwent further change: the tired sixties-style concrete frontage was torn down and a new façade built with finance from the last days of the West Midlands County Council.

At the end of the eighties, as work began on building the best dance facilities in Europe following the purchase of adjacent property in Thorp Street, the door was opened for the creation of the Birmingham Royal Ballet.

Now the Birmingham Hippodrome was really coming into its own.

Above Top: Dame Ninette de Valois lays the Foundation Stone in June 1989 for Birmingham Royal Ballet's new home.
Above Bottom: An artist's impression of the new building, designed by The Seymour Harris Partnership, giving a new look to Thorp Street.

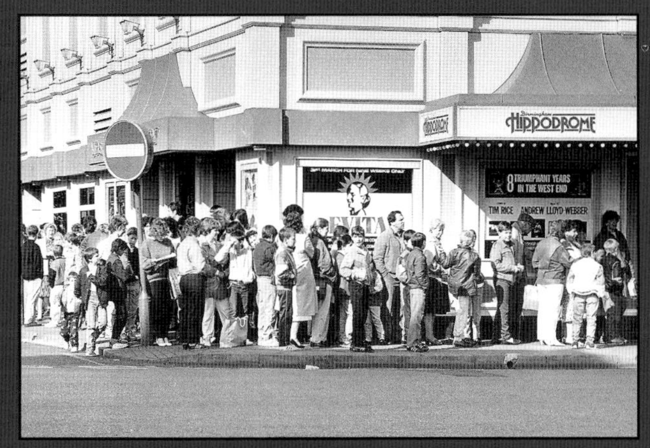

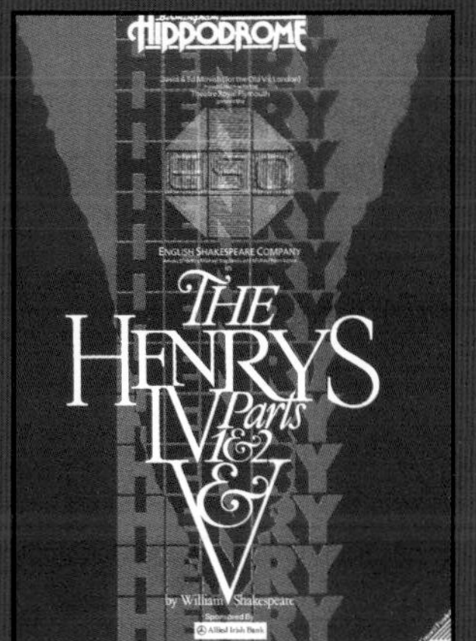

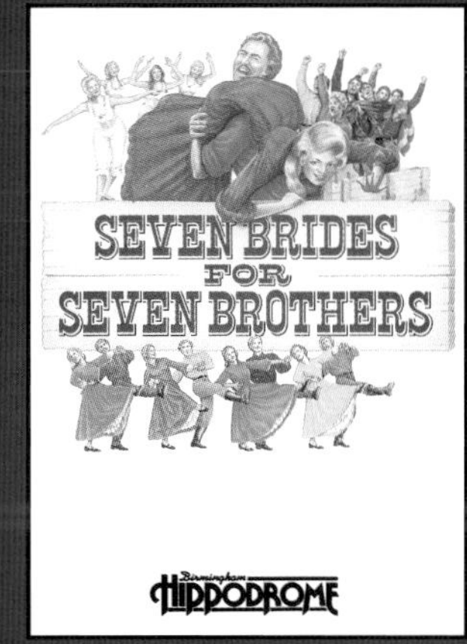

The wide range of entertainment that could be seen at the Hippodrome during the eighties is reflected in the programme covers shown here, as well as a photograph showing the queue for 'Evita' tickets, and the glamorous Harold Fielding production of 'Charlie Girl' with Dora Bryan, Paul Nicholas, Bonnie Langford, Mark Wynter and Nicholas Parsons.

1990 The year of many theatrical disasters: the Savoy Theatre in London was gutted by fire and almost lost; musicals 'Bernadette', 'Someone Like You' and 'King' closed after only a few performances; the Royal Shakespeare Company was forced out of its London homes – the Barbican and Pit – for four months due to lack of funds. An outstanding success was the three Cusack sisters performing in Chekhov's 'Three Sisters' at the Royal Court, London. Glasgow was the European Capital of Culture.
Poll Tax riots in London. East and West Germany reunited. Iraq invaded Kuwait.

1991 **The International Convention Centre, the UK's first purpose-built convention centre, consisting of 11 halls was opened by the Queen.**
Rik Mayall and Adrian Edmondson starred in 'Waiting for Godot' at the Queen's Theatre, London. 'Cats' celebrated its tenth birthday. Nureyev's farewell tour. Dames Margot Fonteyn and Peggy Ashcroft died.
War in the Gulf. After a bungled hard-line coup in the USSR, the communist party fell and the country headed for its first democratic elections in 75 years. Publisher Robert Maxwell drowned mysteriously at sea. Terry Waite was released after spending nearly five years as a hostage in Beirut.

1992 **Meeting of European leaders to discuss ratification of the Maastricht Treaty put the new ICC and Birmingham in front of a pan-European television audience. Second terminal opened at Birmingham International Airport. A partnership agreement was signed with Leipzig.**
'Kiss of the Spider Woman' was the hit of the year. Diana Rigg was outstanding in 'Medea'. Wembley staged the huge production of 'Turandot'. The American Alvin Ailey Dance Company had a season at the London Coliseum.
Drought in the UK reported to be the worst since 1745. Disastrous fire at Windsor Castle.

1993 **Restoration of Victoria Square – opened in May by the Princess of Wales. The Iron Man, a 20 feet high sculpture in**

The Glorious Nineties

From success to success the Hippodrome becomes an unrivalled centre of excellence - including the new home of an international ballet company

THE GLORIOUS NINETIES. No other words will do. The Hippodrome stands unrivalled as it becomes the focal point of the greatest arts coup of the decade: the decision to base the Sadler's Wells Royal Ballet – shortly afterwards to become The Birmingham Royal Ballet – at the theatre.

Peter Wright, director, gives Birmingham its most splendid annual Christmas present: his production of *The Nutcracker*. Like the Hippodrome's pantomimes, which are ever bigger and brighter, it becomes a regular Christmas season feature.

Long cherished dreams become facts. Opera and ballet now have regular seasons. And apart from the Birmingham Royal Ballet and the Welsh National Opera seasons there have been visits from the English National Ballet, Glyndebourne Touring Opera, Scottish Opera and Opera North.

But the Hippodrome is nothing if not a family theatre; and

'Cats', 1995.
The standing ovation for 'Blood Brothers' with Helen Reddy as Mrs Johnstone, 1995.
Below: Phillip Schofield as Joseph, 1994.

now the range is greater and it offers something for everyone.

This, in the nineties, ranges from the outrageous Freddie Starr to Kenneth Branagh and Emma Thompson in *A Midsummer Night's Dream*. From Victoria Wood in *As Seen on TV* to Britt Ekland as seen in pantomime. From Postman Pat to *The Rocky Horror Show*. From Tom Conti in Noël Coward's *Present Laughter* to Ken Dodd presenting his own special brand of laughter.

Sir Andrew Lloyd Webber almost took up residence. After his record breaking run of *Joseph and the Amazing Technicolor Dreamcoat* with Phillip Schofield in 1994, there was the equally phenomenal nine-week season of *Cats* in 1995, followed almost immediately by a third-time-back *Evita*, now starring Marti Webb, which again had the theatre bulging at the seams. He then topped that in 1998 with a hugely successful three-month season of *The Phantom of the Opera* followed in 1999 with what many considered the best production ever seen of *Jesus Christ Superstar*. It came as no surprise to hear that this was the show chosen to see in the Millennium on Broadway.

cast iron by Antony Gormley was unveiled near the Town Hall.
The Gala Season at the Royal Albert Hall by the Bolshoi Ballet was described as the dance event of the century with 160 members of the company dancing to the 90 piece symphony orchestra. 'The Mousetrap' celebrated its 40th birthday. Opera stars Kiri Te Kanawa, Luciano Pavarotti and José Carreras all performed in open-air concerts worldwide.
Peace Treaty was signed between Israel and the Palestinians. Continuing conflicts ravaged the Balkans.

1994 **BMW brought Rover from British Aerospace.**
The Globe Theatre in London was renamed The Gielgud Theatre. John Osborne died. Earls Court staged the rock concert-style show by the American magician/illusionist David Copperfield. Edinburgh Festival Theatre opened, the long-awaited opera house for the Edinburgh International Festival.
After 27 years in prison, Nelson Mandela became president of South Africa. IRA announced cease-fire (subsequently broken and then renewed) as the peace process gathered momentum in Northern Ireland. Earthquake in Kobe, Japan, killed thousands and did untold damage.

1995 **Birmingham became a Sister City of Chicago.**
'Riverdance' was the smash-hit of the year. The show was originally designed as an interlude for the Eurovision Song Contest in Dublin and grew into a full-scale dance event and international attraction. Cameron Mackintosh was knighted. There was a £5 million government cut in funding to the Arts Council. 'Jolson' with Brian Conley opened to great acclaim, winning him a prestigious Laurence Olivier Award.

1996 **The National Sea Life Centre, designed by Sir Norman Foster, was opened. £50 million of National Lottery money from the Millennium Commission kick-started the redevelopment of Digbeth.**
The reconstruction of Shakespeare's Globe Theatre opened on the South Bank of the Thames. 'The Phantom of the Opera' celebrated its 10th birthday.

The new Stephen Joseph Theatre in Scarborough opened with Alan Ayckbourn and Andrew Lloyd Webber's award-winning 'By Jeeves'. Adventures in Motion Pictures' 'Swan Lake', originally presented at Sadler's Wells, moved to the Piccadilly before going to Los Angeles and New York.
New "combination" drug treatments began to win the battle against AIDS.

1997 **A partnership was formed between Birmingham and Johannesburg with a Memorandum of Understanding.**
The Lyceum Theatre reopened in London after more than 50 years during which it served as a Mecca Ballroom and then lay empty while the authorities wrangled over its future. Gerald Kaufman led the Commons Select Committee into the mismanagement of the Royal Opera House, Covent Garden. Donald Sinden was knighted.

1998 **Birmingham hosted the Eurovision Song Contest at the ICC. The G8 meeting held at the ICC with Bill Clinton, Boris Yeltsin and other world leaders attending.**
The National Lottery funded several theatre refurbishments including The Grand Theatre, Wolverhampton. Lenny Henry was awarded the OBE. Birmingham came up trumps at the Olivier Awards with the Birmingham Rep winning the Best New Play Award for 'Frozen' and David Bintley winning the Dance Award for 'The Prospect Before Us' with BRB.
The Good Friday Peace Accord led to the establishment of a new political era in Northern Ireland. Launch of digital broadcasting promised a revolution in television.

1999 **Work began on the Hippodrome 2000 project.**
10th birthday of 'Miss Saigon' at Theatre Royal, Drury Lane.
Launch of the Euro. Preparations for new Scottish Parliament and Welsh Assembly. Hurricanes and earthquakes wreak havoc in Turkey, USA, Greece and Taiwan.
On 29th November Her Majesty the Queen attends the Royal Variety Performance at the Birmingham Hippodrome.

'Les Misérables', 1997.

Andrew Lloyd Webber has been the dominant figure in the development of the British musical in the second half of the twentieth century.

His career started modestly enough when he met the young Tim Rice and together they wrote a thirty minute end-of-term school concert called *Joseph and the Amazing Technicolor Dreamcoat*.

It was this self-same *Joseph*, albeit on a much grander scale, which opened yet another chapter of the Hippodrome's history when, in 1994, it became the first show to take more than £1 million on the first day of advance booking.

However, back to the theatre itself. In 1992 the stalls were re-raked to improve comfort and sightlines for the audiences.

So what now of the future? The Birmingham Hippodrome stands for the best – and you can be assured that the best is yet to come, with the management of the Hippodrome spending four years in the nineties preparing and planning its own next century with the ambitious Hippodrome 2000 project.

Gary Wilmot starred in the hugely successful 'The Goodbye Girl' alongside Marti Webb, in 1998. Earlier he had starred in 'Me and My Girl' with Jessica Martin.

Brian Conley as Jolson, which was seen at the Hippodrome before a sensational London run, scooping all the awards before starting a worldwide tour. Opposite: 'The Phantom of The Opera'.

Birmingham
HIPPODROME
WEDNESDAY 24TH JUNE-
THURSDAY 24TH SEPTEMBER 1998

Birmingham Royal Ballet

1931 Ninette de Valois founded a company at Sadler's Wells Theatre. It was known as The Vic-Wells Ballet, as it performed both at Sadler's Wells Theatre and the Old Vic Theatre in London.

1940 Sadler's Wells Theatre was bombed during the war and consequently the Company began to tour widely throughout the country. The name of the Company changed to The Sadler's Wells Ballet.

1946 The Company was invited to become the resident company of the Royal Opera House, Covent Garden. Dame Ninette therefore decided to found a second Company first called Sadler's Wells Opera Ballet and subsequently renamed Sadler's Wells Theatre Ballet at Sadler's Wells Theatre.

1951 Sadler's Wells Theatre Ballet undertook a highly successful tour of the USA.

1955 Sadler's Wells Theatre Ballet temporarily lost its links with Sadler's Wells Theatre and based itself with its sister company at the Royal Opera House.

1956 A Royal Charter was bestowed on both Companies and their joint school. The Sadler's Wells Ballet became The Royal Ballet and Sadler's Wells Theatre Ballet became known as The Touring Company of The Royal Ballet. First Birmingham performances at the Alexandra Theatre by the Touring Company.

1970 The Touring Company returned to its base at Sadler's Wells Theatre, whilst continuing to tour the country. They gave their first performance at the Birmingham Hippodrome

Anne Sacks of the London Evening Standard takes a look at the ballet company that has made Birmingham its home.

BIRMINGHAM ROYAL BALLET has had a chequered history but now, thanks to a stable home at the Hippodrome, it enjoys a golden age of creativity. It was not always so. There have been ups and downs in the 53 years since the company was founded but its consolidation is due to Sir Peter Wright who, as Artistic Director, achieved his ambition to transplant to Birmingham. Under his successor, David Bintley, BRB has become the premier ballet company in Britain.

Bintley is making a truly creative mark as a choreographer. He has already created an impressive range of ballets in the English tradition of theatricality, in which dance is used to advance the narrative or illuminate character or situation. He has also forged a style of his own that is elegant and pure and captures a modern spirit.

As leader of BRB, his achievements are equally impressive.

From David Bintley's ''Still Life' at the Penguin Café', 1996 Joseph Cipolla as Southern Cape Zebra.

From Sir Peter Wright's production of 'The Sleeping Beauty', 1997 Marion Tait as Carabosse

Through his own productivity, imagination and dedication, he has established Birmingham as the new capital of British ballet. Since his appointment in 1995, the City has become an unrivalled centre for creativity in dance with exciting new works by Bintley himself and guest choreographers invited by him. There is no other ballet company in the country that is supplying its dancers with such an abundance of new roles to challenge and stimulate them. These ballets, always performed to the highest standards, have attracted a keen new audience, which comes to Birmingham from all over the Midlands. Building a new audience for ballet in a hostile climate, where ballet is wrongly judged as élitist, is in itself a remarkable achievement. The company is now a great source of civic pride.

Because of the emphasis on creativity, the present company reflects the company that began in 1946 when The Sadler's Wells Ballet left Sadler's Wells Theatre in north London for the Royal Opera House in Covent Garden. That left a gap, which the indomitable Ninette de Valois, founder of the company, determined to fill. So she created the Sadler's Wells Opera Ballet, whose role was to provide dancers for the popular Sadler's Wells Opera. Never short of ambition, de Valois decided the fledgling company should act as a nursery for young dancers and choreographers.

So Peggy van Praagh was put in charge – and created an instant success. The next year (1947) the company became Sadler's Wells Theatre Ballet and entered a period of ten years that were to lay the foundations of the modern company. Creativity flourished. The vitality of dancers such as Svetlana Beriosova and the choreography of John Cranko and Kenneth MacMillan set a style and character for the company. It was lively, popular and

1977	The Touring Company changed its name to Sadler's Wells Royal Ballet, with Peter Wright as Director. David Bintley's first professional work 'The Outsider' premiered at Birmingham Hippodrome and he became resident choreographer for Sadler's Wells Royal Ballet.
1987	Initial soundings between the Royal Opera House, Arts Council and Birmingham about the feasibility of Sadler's Wells Royal Ballet relocating to Birmingham.
1989	The City of Birmingham invited Sadler's Wells Royal Ballet to relocate to the City. 'Hobson's Choice' was created for Sadler's Wells Royal Ballet by David Bintley.
1990	Sadler's Wells Royal Ballet moved to its new home at the Birmingham Hippodrome and changed its name to The Birmingham Royal Ballet.
1995	The 1995/96 Season saw an exciting transition from the directorship of Sir Peter Wright to the new Artistic Director, David Bintley.
1996	Birmingham Royal Ballet continued to tour the United Kingdom and overseas, presenting a diverse range of classical ballet and new works.
1997	Birmingham Royal Ballet became independent of The Royal Opera House.
1999	David Bintley made further commitment to the Birmingham Royal Ballet by announcing that he would remain as Artistic Director amid speculation that he would be the next to lead The Royal Ballet.

THEATRES AT WHICH BIRMINGHAM ROYAL BALLET PERFORM

Alhambra Theatre, Bradford
Empire Theatre, Sunderland
Theatre Royal, Plymouth
Royal Opera House, London
Lowry Centre, Salford,

BIRMINGHAM ROYAL BALLET ABROAD

1992	Far East
1993	Italy
1995	Germany and Japan
1996	Sicily
1998	South Africa
2000	Hong Kong, New York and Chicago

Above left:* *'Swan Lake', Leticia Müller as Odette, 1995.
Above right:* *'The Nutcracker Sweeties', Joseph Cipolla and Chenca Williams – choreographed by David Bintley to music by Duke Ellington, 1996.

adventurous – the nursery had turned into a glittering showcase for British talent. The company won over audiences at home and abroad with small-scale versions of the classics and revivals too small for an opera house such as de Valois' 'Rake's Progress'.

So successful was the first regional tour of this energetic adolescent that in 1956 John Field was appointed to take it into an era of distinction. It became the official touring arm of The Royal Ballet and the company enlarged to focus on classics, which toured regions for the first time. Its stars, including Doreen Wells and David Wall, became as famous and as adored as any at Covent Garden. It filled theatres in the regions and in Europe and North America. The trouble was that it had become a duplication of the Covent Garden company and the expense of touring became a financial burden to the Royal Opera House.

So the company was disbanded and replaced by an "experimental" group called The Royal Ballet New Group, directed

Above: Michael O'Hare and Leticia Müller in 'Hobson's Choice', 1996.
Right: Dorcas Walters, David Justin and Robert Parker in
'The Protecting Veil', 1998. Both productions by David Bintley.

by Peter Wright. Its failure was almost immediate. The tradition of Royal Ballet productions was far too strong to be replaced in this unorthodox way.

However, Peter Wright refused to be fazed by this setback. He was a visionary leader whose mission it became to rebuild the company as a powerful force in British ballet. In 1973 the company size was restored to 50 dancers. Wright strongly believed that the company could only thrive if it had a permanent base. It moved, therefore, into Sadler's Wells Theatre and in 1977 became Sadler's Wells Royal Ballet, consolidating its wide-ranging repertory and high performing standards.

Once again, it became a company in its own right, similar to the creative first company of 1946, except larger and improved. In the 1980s it sparkled with dancers including Marion Tait and Miyako Yoshida while David Bintley stepped into the shoes of Cranko and MacMillan as the choreographic force.

***Above top:* Sir Peter Wright handing over the artist directorship to David Bintley, 1995.**
***Above:* 'Edward II', Wolfgang Stollwitzer as Edward II, 1997.**
***Above right:* 'Giselle', 1999.**
***Opposite:* 'The Sleeping Beauty', Leticia Müller as Princess Aurora in Sir Peter Wright's production stunningly designed by Philip Prowse, 1997.**

In the late 1980s, Wright stunned the ballet world by announcing the company was moving to Birmingham. This provoked an outcry, fuelled by the London and national press. Dancers were reluctant to move and sceptics did not believe there was an audience for ballet in Birmingham. They called it absurd. But Wright knew that a permanent base and quality facilities were secrets of success. As promised, a national cultural institution was transplanted in 1990 and renamed Birmingham Royal Ballet. Birmingham City Council and the Hippodrome have been its strongest supporters, a relationship that continues today, bolstered by generous local sponsors.

Wright was due to retire but decided to stay on to settle in the company. In 1995, he handed over the Artistic Directorship to David Bintley, whom he had nurtured a decade before in the Sadler's Wells days. In only five years, Bintley has created an era of pre-eminence. The company that was started as a little sister to the Covent Garden company has eclipsed it to dominate British ballet. If Wright built a new audience for ballet in the Midlands, Bintley expanded it. There is a buzz in the Hippodrome on ballet nights and the home that it offers makes a large contribution to BRB's golden age.

Welsh National Opera

Simon Rees, dramaturg for Welsh National Opera explains how Birmingham Hippodrome has, since the 1960s, been the principal touring venue for WNO in England

1943	A group of music lovers met to discuss the foundation of a company to produce grand opera in Wales.
1946	After two and a half years of preparation, Welsh National Opera staged its first production – a double bill of 'Cavalleria rusticana' & 'Pagliacci' at the Prince of Wales Theatre, Cardiff. It was followed the next evening by 'Faust'.
1948	To supplement the amateur chorus based in Cardiff, a second chorus was established in Swansea covering Swansea, West Wales and Mid Wales. The unique quality of sound based on the great Welsh choral tradition of chapel and community choirs was already beginning to attract attention.
1950	Charles Mackerras made his début with the company.
1952	The company performed 'Nabucco' which had not been seen in Britain for over 100 years. It was to become something of a signature production for WNO.
1961	Charles Groves became Musical Director (until 1963).
1968	James Lockhart left Covent Garden to become Musical Director at WNO where he stayed until 1973. The long awaited professionalisation of the company began. Under Lockhart the list of contract principals was impressive – Thomas Allen, Josephine Barstow, Ramon Remedios, Richard Van Allan, Stuart Burrows, Margaret Price. James Levine made his British conducting début in 'Aida'. The company made its first visit to Birmingham, performing at the Alexandra Theatre. A professional chorus was formed. Some of the amateur choristers auditioned successfully and gave up their jobs as miners, steelworkers and storekeepers. The voluntary chorus was still used for some of the larger-scale work.
1970	Full-time professional orchestra for WNO was launched – initially called the Welsh Philharmonia. John Stein, leader of the Royal Ballet, was enticed to Cardiff as leader, a post he still holds today.

OPERA HAS BEEN PERFORMED in Birmingham for a surprisingly long time: since the middle of the 18th century, visiting companies have been coming to the city to put on touring productions of operas, with theatres in Moor Street, King Street and New Street being the earliest venues. Birmingham has never had its own full-scale full-time opera company (although in recent years the City of Birmingham Touring Opera under the direction of Graham Vick has done some remarkable work) and the City continues to rely on visiting companies to provide it with the opera it so enthusiastically consumes.

The company with the largest touring presence in Birmingham is, and has for a long time been, the Cardiff-based Welsh National Opera. Welsh National Opera was founded in 1946 by a group of amateur musicians in Cardiff and Swansea, who put together an amateur chorus and hired both professional

'Idomeneo', 1995, with Rebecca Evans, Suzanne Murphy and Dennis O'Neill

and amateur soloists and a series of professional orchestras, before becoming fully professional with an orchestra of its own in 1969. Welsh National Opera began touring from its earliest years, and its first visit to Birmingham came in October 1968, with a season at the Alexandra Theatre. By this time the company's professional status was well known, and London critics were already used to expecting the highest standards, especially from the famous Chorus and particularly in the Verdi repertory with which the company had made its name.

It was in November 1971 that Welsh National Opera first came to the Birmingham Hippodrome, with a season made up of *The Magic Flute*, *Boris Godunov*, *Aida* and *Lulu*, a programme that significantly covers nearly two hundred years of opera, and an important sample of WNO's ability to work both in classical repertory and in the modern field with Berg's masterpiece. The

'La Traviata', 1995, with WNO chorus

following year saw *Turandot*, *Don Giovanni*, *Rigoletto* and *Billy Budd*, and from that time on WNO's appearances at the Birmingham Hippodrome became a regular feature of the theatre's programming.

One of Brian McMaster's first actions on taking over as WNO's General Administrator in 1976 was to rationalise the touring programme, so that the clashes that had happened in the past, with three companies producing *La Bohème* within thirty miles of one another, should no longer occur! At the same time, WNO declared that the Birmingham Hippodrome was to be the company's English headquarters. This simply meant that there was office space available within the Hippodrome for the co-ordination of some of the company's ancillary activities. The most important of these was the establishment of the Birmingham branch of Friends of WNO, developed by Howard Lichterman

'Nabucco', 1995, with Janice Cairns

1971	The Hippodrome welcomed WNO for the first time.
1973	The chorus became fully professional. WNO undertook its first foreign tour with performances of 'Billy Budd' in Lausanne and Zurich. Since then the company has performed throughout Europe and also in New York and Japan.
1976	In a re-organisation of its touring, WNO declared Birmingham its English headquarters. The Hippodrome offered office space to co-ordinate some of the company's ancillary activities.
1977	The Birmingham branch of the Friends of Welsh National Opera was established.
1980	With the Hippodrome closed for refurbishment, WNO transferred to Coventry. Sponsorship from Amoco, WNO's new, and to be long-standing, business sponsor paid for patrons to be bused from Birmingham.
1986	The legendary Theatre Director Peter Stein accepted an invitation to work with WNO. His 'Otello' attracted interest from around the world. Later that year the complete 'Ring Cycle' was performed in Wales for the first time. WNO took it to London for the first visit by a regional company to Covent Garden.
1987	Sir Charles Mackerras became Musical Director beginning his tenure with a magnificent production of 'The Trojans'.
1992	WNO's current Musical Director, Carlo Rizzi joined the company.
1995	WNO began its 50th Anniversary season with a new production of 'Nabucco'.
1996	The Company celebrated its first 50 years with new productions of the first operas the Company performed – 'Cavalleria rusticana', 'Pagliacci' and 'Faust'.
1999	The Company won a grand slam of opera awards for its work during the previous year: a Barclays Theatre Award; Laurence Olivier Award; Royal Philharmonic Society Award and Evening Standard Award.

Left: 'Beatrice and Benedict', 1994, with Donald Maxwell.
Below: 'The Coronation of Poppea', 1997, with Catrin Wyn-Davies, Linda Kitchen, Neil Jenkins and Paul Nilon.

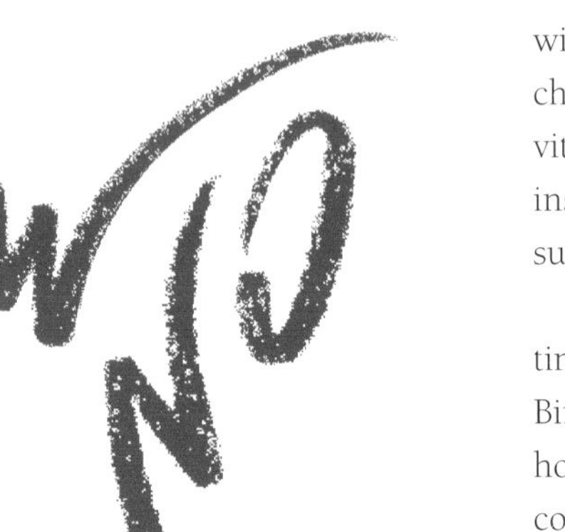

with Rene Lee and a group of volunteers. This branch, now chaired by Birmingham solicitor and musicologist Chris Ball, is vital to the work of WNO's Friends as a whole, and has been instrumental in many fund-raising projects in enthusiastic support of numerous productions.

Richard Fawkes, in his history of WNO, records that for a time there was a rumour that WNO would move its operation to Birmingham, as the company had failed to find a permanent home in Cardiff, but this rumour was not in fact true. The company had been disappointed at not being able to take over Cardiff's Capital Theatre but, then as now, the company's home has remained in the Welsh capital.

The one year which did not see WNO at the Hippodrome was 1980, when the theatre was closed for a major refit. WNO went to Coventry instead, and a grant from Amoco underwrote the week and provided funding for busing patrons from Birmingham. This was Amoco's first regional Festival of Opera, and it led to many more, confirming Amoco's relationship with WNO as a major sponsorship partner.

In recent years, WNO has continued to regard the Birmingham Hippodrome as its principal English touring venue. Productions that have been given with particular success have included Wagner's *Ring Cycle* that began in 1983, with other productions by Göran Järvefelt (*La Traviata*, *Un ballo in maschera* and *The Magic Flute*) making frequent reappearances; the four productions by Peter Stein (*Otello*, *Falstaff*, *Pelléas et Mélisande* and *Peter Grimes*) of which *Pelléas* could only be revived at the Hippodrome because of the theatre's superior backstage facilities; Joachim Herz's *Madam Butterfly* is a regular favourite with its exquisite set and costumes; and recent scandalous successes such as David Alden's production of *The Coronation of Poppea*, with its lollipop-coloured sets are a psychedelic slant on Ancient Rome!

Clockwise (from top left): 'Iphigénie en Tauride' 1992, with Diana Montague; 'Madam Butterfly' 1978, with John Treleaven and Magdalena Falewicz; 'Falstaff', 1988, with Donald Maxwell; 'Carmen', 1998, with Sara Fulgoni.

Musical Spectrum of the last 20 years

The world of musicals is full of colour, spectacle and drama and the Hippodrome has built a national reputation for staging the biggest and the best.

THE TYPE OF THEATRE available to Birmingham theatregoers today is diverse and eclectic: many strands exist simultaneously across every size and style of venue but, in the competitive world of show business, the most popular has been the musicals. The Hippodrome is the best stage for the costly blockbuster musicals: technically advanced and with an auditorium offering today's international impresarios the highest-grossing cash potential in the Midlands. The boldest and most lavish musicals have, therefore, been a feature at the Hippodrome for over fifty years now and, some would say, have replaced plays as the mainstream of British theatre because they have brought back the mass audience.

From the 1930s, remarkable "book" musicals from the golden age of Broadway dominated, with their frivolous and often silly stories, popular songs, hypnotic lyrics and melodies. The

Opposite page: 'The Blues Brothers' has appeared frequently since 1993. 'Annie' starring Lesley Joseph, 1999. This page: 'Crazy For You' 1996. 'Evita', was a huge success on both visits to the Hippodrome. 'Buddy - The Buddy Holly Story' played in 1991 and again in 1996. 'Me and My Girl' with Gary Wilmot and Jessica Martin in 1994.

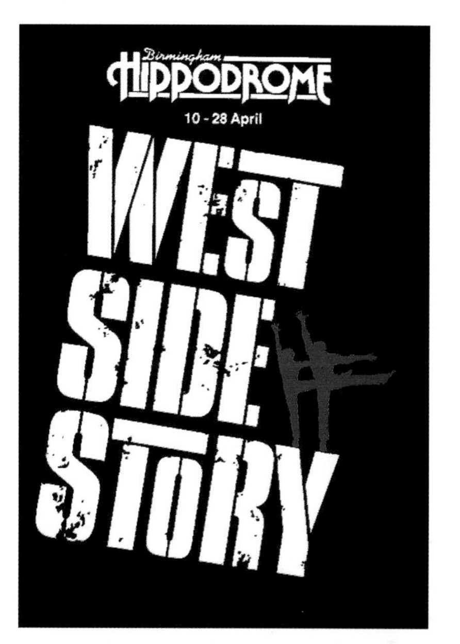

work of composers Irving Berlin, Jerome Kern, George Gershwin, Ivor Novello, Cole Porter and Richard Rodgers was frequently staged at the Hippodrome, both professionally and by amateur companies. After the 1950s Lerner and Loewe hit *My Fair Lady*, a turning point was the mid-1960s, an innocent era which produced the optimism of *Fiddler On The Roof* and *Hello, Dolly!* – the last solid hits from the old school which followed the traditional formula of blending comedy, sentiment and romance with a succession of hit songs and dance.

Taking advantage of the post-censorship era, the hippy rock musical *Hair* was the turning point of the new musicals for many Birmingham theatregoers – with its background of drug use, civil disobedience, brief nudity and the "new age rhythm".

The Hippodrome's fortunes were revitalised by the start of Tim Rice and Andrew Lloyd Webber's collaboration in the biblical

'Joseph and the Amazing Technicolor Dreamcoat', a regular favourite. 'Martin Guerre' 1999. Paul Nicholas in 'The Pirates of Penzance' 1989. 'Show Boat', 1990.

rock-anthem musical *Joseph and the Amazing Technicolor Dreamcoat*. This has been much revived here in the past thirty years, often produced by Bill Kenwright, one of the few producers with continuous commitment to the health of theatre outside London (as well as a passion for Everton Football Club!). It was followed by *Jesus Christ Superstar*, using the same palette, including haunting laments, and *Evita*, based on the career of Eva Peron with more memorable tunes including 'Don't Cry for Me, Argentina'. The technical standards of these shows were to become the hallmark of later productions by Lloyd Webber and his involvement with Cameron Mackintosh, with *Cats* and *Phantom of the Opera*, with their convention-challenging subject matter, innovative use of music and sophisticated concepts in design and staging.

These shows – together with Tommy Steele's *Hans Andersen* and *Singin' in the Rain* (in which he also starred for the impresario and Hippodrome friend Harold Fielding), Willy Russell's tough and unsentimental *Blood Brothers* (another Bill Kenwright production), the rejuvenated old movie *42nd Street*, the reworking of *Me and my Girl* and the vivacious *Crazy for You*, through to Schönberg and Boublil's full-length *Les Misérables* and *Martin Guerre* (both produced by Cameron Mackintosh) – amounted to a new artistic stature for the British musical without forsaking its traditional appeal.

The Hippodrome has been fortunate in staging them all, as originally conceived, often for long runs, and without the paring down frequently seen on tours in the provinces. Their producers, including Harold Fielding, Bill Kenwright, David Pugh, André Ptaszynski, Cameron Mackintosh and Paul Elliott – have, in collaboration with the good judgement of theatre director, Peter Tod, improved the status of the Hippodrome as a theatrical institution and thriving business, with a splendid response from Birmingham theatregoers.

Clockwise: 'Carmen Jones', 1994. 'The Phantom of The Opera' made its mark in 1998. 'Return to the Forbidden Planet', 1996. 'Five Guys Named Moe', 1996. 'Les Misérables' from 1997. 'Oklahoma!' 1980.

Pantomime at "The Hipp"

1958-59
ROBINSON CRUSOE
with David Whitfield, Hermene French, Roy Parry.

1959-60
ALADDIN
with Norman Evans, Dickie Valentine, Eve Boswell.

1961-62
THE SLEEPING BEAUTY
with Lonnie Donegan, The Three Monarchs, Danny La Rue, Alan Haynes.

1962-63
ROBINSON CRUSOE
with Norman Wisdom.

1963-64
PUSS IN BOOTS
with Frankie Vaughan, The Three Monarchs and George Moon.

1965-66
HUMPTY DUMPTY
the all-time record breaker with Ken Dodd, Ken Roberts, Judy Collins, Iris Sadler.

1966-67
THE SLEEPING BEAUTY
with Morecambe and Wise, Eddie Malloy, Kevin Scott.

1967-68
ALADDIN
with Harry Worth, Dana, Peter Butterworth.

1968-69
CINDERELLA
with Des O'Connor, Freddie Starr, Jack Douglas, Dennis Lotis.

1969-70
BABES IN THE WOOD
with Mike and Bernie Winters, Wyn Calvin.

1970-71
DICK WHITTINGTON
with Freddie Davies, Anita Harris, Billy Dainty.

1971-72
JACK AND THE BEANSTALK
with The Bachelors, Frank Carson and Birmingham's then up-and-coming Don Maclean.

1972-73
CINDERELLA
with Dickie Henderson, Arthur Askey.

"Three things are required at Christmas time, Plum Pudding, Beef and Pantomime, Folks could resist the former two, Without the latter none could do".

The Birmingham Hippodrome was something of a latecomer to the pantomime stakes – but soon caught up! Today it is the nation's pantomime flagship, breaking UK box office records and producing shows in association with Paul Elliott, the King of Panto himself, which are seen all over the country.

In earlier days the pantos had previously been staged at the London Palladium or elsewhere. Today the shows are brand new and the situation is reversed: by virtue of its successes, the Hippodrome has become England's ambassador of panto, sending out messages of goodwill every Christmas.

The first pantomime, after many years of ice pageants and other Christmas Variety shows, arrived in 1957 at the Hippodrome in the shape of *Jack and the Beanstalk* with Beryl Reid, Coventry's Reg Dixon and Audrey Jeans. It was a show originally destined for the Theatre Royal in New Street, a theatre which

Above: Des O'Connor with the children from 'Cinderella', 1968/69

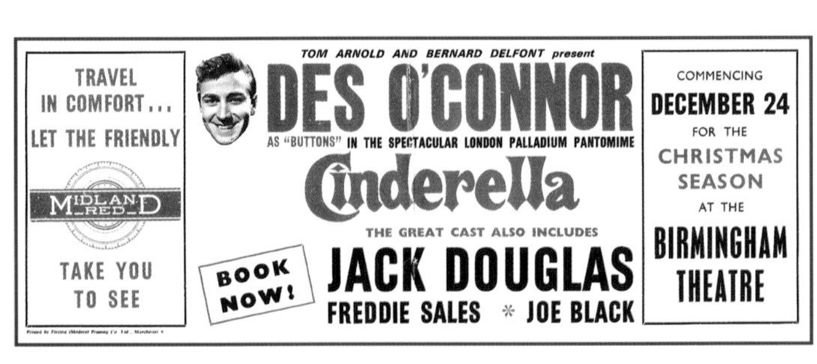

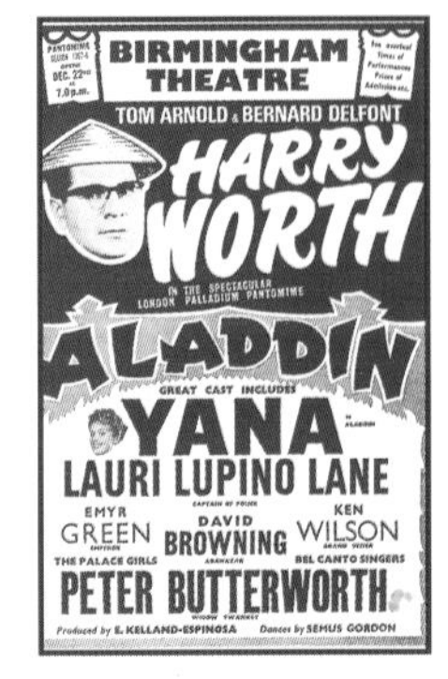

Les Dawson.

Dickie Henderson

Arthur Askey

Norman Wisdom

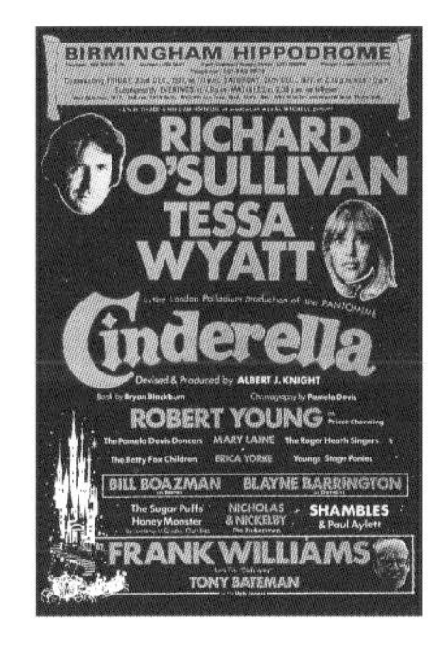

Left: Billy Dainty, one of the great pantomime dames.

became one of the first victims of Birmingham's real-estate boom of the fifties when the sites they stood on were more valuable than the buildings themselves.

But it's an ill wind... and the loss of the Theatre Royal proved to be the Hippodrome's saviour; pantomime becoming a key ingredient of the Hippodrome's annual programme.

1973-74
ROBINSON CRUSOE
with Charlie Williams, Roy Hudd, Billy Whittaker.

1974-75
ALADDIN
with Larry Grayson, Alfred Marks, Dilys Watling.

1975-76
PETER PAN
with Alan Curtis, Elizabeth Norman followed by a two week run of **EMU IN PANTOLAND** *with Rod Hull and Billy Dainty.*

1976-77
JACK AND THE BEANSTALK
with Charlie Drake, Alan Randall.

1977-78
CINDERELLA
with Richard O'Sullivan, Tessa Wyatt.

1978-79
TURN AGAIN WHITTINGTON
with Norman Wisdom.

1979-80
BABES IN THE WOOD
with Les Dawson, Roger de Courcey and Nookie Bear.

1981-82
ALADDIN
with Danny La Rue.

1982-83
DICK WHITTINGTON
with The Krankies, Paul Henry, Billy Dainty.

1983-84
JACK AND THE BEANSTALK
with Cilla Black, Paul Squire, Harry Worth, Gareth Hunt, Jimmy Cricket.

1984-85
CANNON AND BALL CHRISTMAS SPECTACULAR
with Tommy Cannon and Bobby Ball, Marti Caine, Brian Marshall.

1985-86
HUMPTY DUMPTY
with Keith Harris and Orville, Norman Collier, Windsor Davies, Rustie Lee, Stuart Gasston.

Paul Elliott gives his "Ugly Sister" a contract!

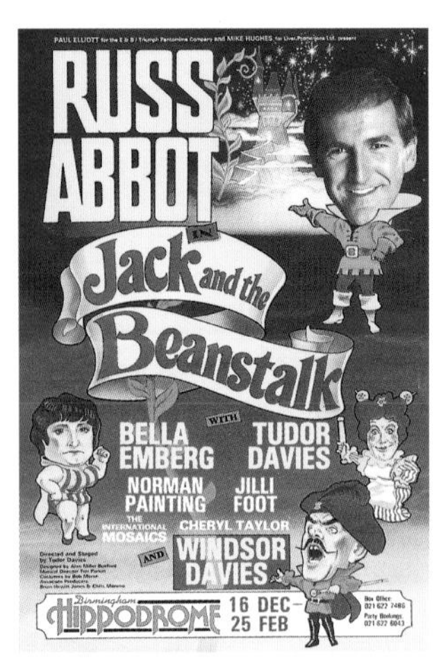

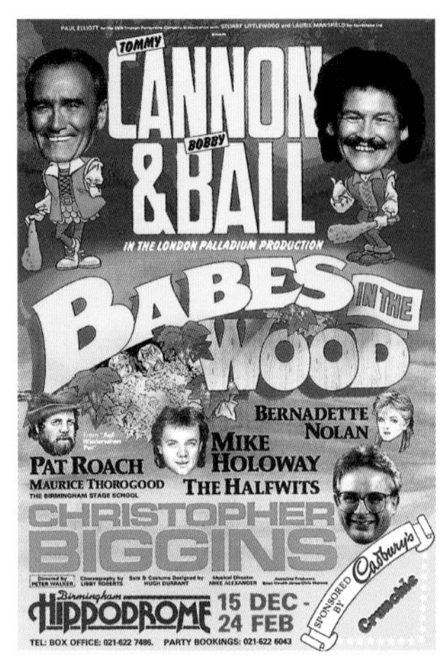

'Aladdin', 1992/93

The beginning of a new pantomime era began in 1988, when impresario Paul Elliott started producing the Hippodrome's annual pantomimes, which have all been co-produced by Peter Tod, the Hippodrome's Theatre Director, and the majority directed and choreographed by Carole Todd.

'Jack and the Beanstalk', 1988/89.

'Aladdin', 1992/93

Right: Danny La Rue in 'Cinderella', 1998/99

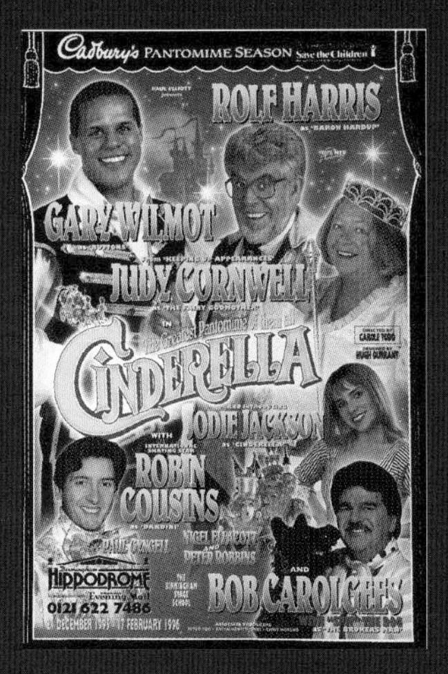

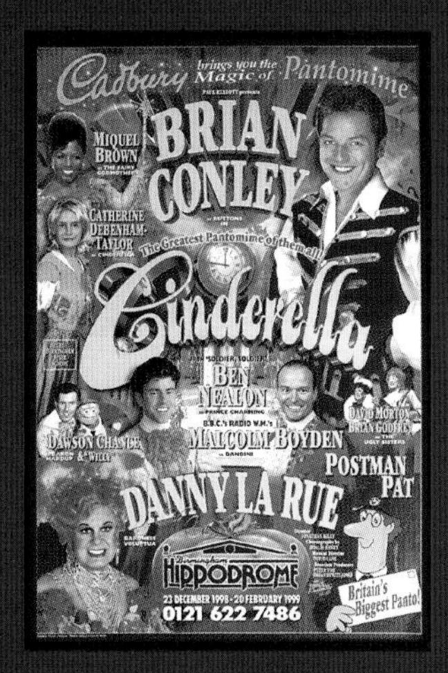

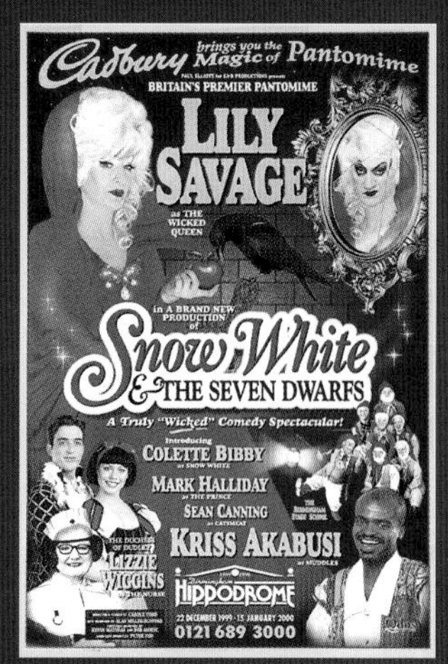

'Dick Whittington', 1993/94

Above and right: 'Mother Goose', 1996/97

Left: 'Jack and the Beanstalk', 1994/95

Above and right: 'Goldilocks and the 3 Bears' 1997/98

'Cinderella', 1995/96

'Snow White and the Seven Dwarfs', 1999/2000

Theatregoers of Tomorrow

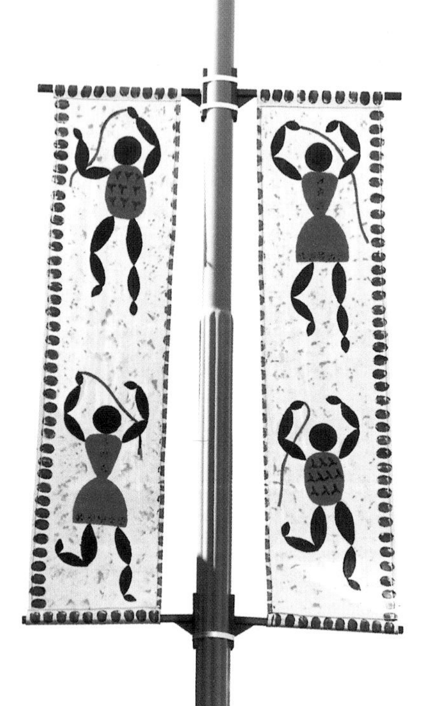

The important relationship which has been built between the Hippodrome and young people.

CHILDREN AND YOUNG people have, of course, made up a significant part of the Hippodrome's audience throughout its history. In the last fifteen years, however, the theatre has played a pioneering role in education and outreach work, through a wide range of imaginative and challenging projects. Thousands of young people have been involved in work alongside productions, creating their own drama and dance, collaborating with professionals at the theatre or in their schools.

In 1984, Sadlers Wells Royal Ballet based a Special Projects Development Officer at the Birmingham Hippodrome, and began co-ordination of ballet projects, which were already well established by the time the company re-located. As Birmingham Royal Ballet, they have continued with an outreach programme that is of the highest possible quality.

Then, in 1988, the Hippodrome set up an Education Department – the first of its kind in a British Touring Theatre. Under the new Education Liaison Officer, Pepita Hanna, major projects have included the 'Theatre is the Place To Be' video pack, a full-scale community opera *Of Bricks and Bones*, and numerous projects with schools across the whole age range.

In the last ten years, the theatre has again led the way, in running substantial projects alongside the major musicals, with hundreds of schools involved in work alongside *Cats*, *Les Misérables* and *The Phantom of the Opera*. A special 'Introduction to Pantomime Roadshow' has been commissioned and has

successfully toured primary schools in the autumn term over the last three years. Original packs and projects have been created for Pantomime, as well as for the long-standing collaboration with leading children's theatre company, Whirligig.

The new development of the theatre places education even closer to the heart of the Hippodrome's activities and will improve still further the resources for outreach projects. For every young member of the Hippodrome's audience, the visit to the theatre can contain real magic which will remain with them for life. The aim of the theatre's education and outreach work is to support this, to encourage substantial and active involvement in the theatre, and to ensure that as many young people as possible have the opportunity to be touched by the magic of theatre.

The experience and opportunity of the Hippodrome and Birmingham Royal Ballet's Educational Projects in workshops, rehearsal, on stage and (below right) in their own schools with the Pantomime Roadshow.

Theatres of Birmingham

Birmingham's existing theatres

BIRMINGHAM HIPPODROME, Hurst Street
Opened 1899 Current use: Theatre

ALEXANDRA THEATRE, Station Street
Opened 1901 Current use: Theatre

OLD REP, Station Street
Opened 1913 Current use: Theatre

CRESCENT THEATRE, Sheepcote Street (1998)
(originally sited in Cambridge Street before moving to Cumberland Street in 1964)
Opened 1932 Current use: Amateur Theatre

HIGHBURY LITTLE THEATRE, Sutton Coldfield
Opened 1942 Current use: Amateur Theatre

HALL GREEN LITTLE THEATRE
Opened 1951 Current use: Amateur Theatre

SUTTON ARTS THEATRE, Sutton Coldfield
Opened 1954 Current use: Amateur Theatre

MIDLANDS ARTS CENTRE, Cannon Hill
Opened 1962 Current use: Theatre/Cinema

BIRMINGHAM REP, Broad Street
Opened 1971 Current use: Theatre

THE DRUM, Aston
Opened 1998 Current use: Performance space

Down the centuries, theatres have played an important role in the life of the City. Some are lost and some are gone forever, but Birmingham still proudly boasts some of the country's finest.

THE CITY'S first theatre was constructed in 1730 in a yard between High Street and Moor Street. Ten years later it was reconstructed as the Moor Street Theatre attracting professional companies of actors from London. When the King Street Theatre opened in 1751 it gradually captured the audience from Moor Street, and by 1764 there was again only one theatre in the town. With the construction of the Theatre Royal in the 1770s, history repeated itself and within a few years it had the (unofficial) monopoly which it maintained effectively until the 1850s. Then suddenly there was an explosion of new building and enterprise. Concert-halls, music-halls, playhouses and variety palaces sprang up across City. By the end of the century when the Hippodrome opened, Birmingham was awash with theatrical entertainment.

The Alexandra Theatre

Opened in 1901 as the Lyceum, but was renamed in honour of the Queen one year later when it was taken over by Lester Collingwood, who was killed in an early car accident. The theatre passed into the hands of Leon Salberg who subsequently formed the Alexandra Repertory Company which performed there from 1927 until 1974. The building was rebuilt in 1935 and when Leon died three years later, his son Derek took over as director, establishing himself as one of the all-time great theatrical personalities in the City. His family continued to own the theatre, struggling against cost, until the Alex was bought by the Apollo Leisure Group in 1995, which in 1999 came under the control of the American SFX Corporation.

Aston Hippodrome

Opened off High Street, Aston in 1908. Throughout its life it was essentially a variety theatre. Following a fire in 1938, it was substantially rebuilt. Having survived the war and the 1950s, the Aston Hippodrome closed its doors in 1960. For a while thereafter it was used as a bingo hall (from 1967), but that too closed and the building was demolished in 1980.

On this site The Drum opened its doors in 1998 as a mixed programme venue for visual and performing arts. It aims to establish itself as the UK's first Black Arts Centre reflecting the artistic and cultural activities of the Black, African, Asian and Caribbean people.

Aston Theatre Royal

Opened in 1893, but almost immediately ran into financial troubles and was sold the following year to Charles Bernard who partially redesigned the auditorium and ran it as a playhouse. The building was substantially refurbished in 1912, but closed again in 1926, reopening the following year as the Astoria Cinema. In 1955 it was transformed into Alpha TV Studios, which in 1967 became part of ATV, (who had the ITV franchise for the Midlands).

Birmingham Repertory Theatre

Opened 1971, the Birmingham Repertory Company moved to Broad Street into a building which was hailed at the time by 'Plays and Players' magazine as "the first truly modern theatre in England". The Rep Company continues to stage world-class productions of classics and modern works in the main house. Its studio, now renamed The Door, presents contemporary work. Both auditoria were substantially refurbished throughout the summer of 1999.

The Carlton Theatre

Opened in Saltley in July 1900 by Arthur Carlton as a variety theatre. In 1907 it changed hands and, four years later, the name was changed to Birmingham Coliseum and Gaiety. In 1921 it was turned into a picture palace and remained so until its closure in the early 1940s.

The Crescent Theatre

The original Crescent Theatre opened in Cambridge Street in 1932, a conversion of several houses and a hall. In 1964, after much fund-raising, the resident amateur company was able to have a purpose-built theatre, constructed in Cumberland Street, where they remained until 1998 when they moved to a new building in Sheepcote Street, part of the Brindleyplace development.

The Empire Theatre

Opened in 1894, was designed by Frank Matcham and stood on the site of the former Day's Crystal Palace Concert Hall, close to the Hippodrome, on the corner of Hurst Street and Smallbrook (Queensway). Its owners, Moss Empires, claimed it was "the most beautiful variety theatre in England", and it was certainly popular with the public. The Empire was badly damaged by enemy bombing in 1941 and was demolished completely ten years later.

The Gaiety

Opened in Coleshill Street in 1846 as Holders Hotel and Concert Hall. Over the next fifty years it had several changes of owner and almost as many changes of name. It ran as the Gaiety Theatre of Varieties, a well-known and well-regarded music-hall seating 3,500 people, from 1897 until it closed in 1920. The building was subsequently used as a cinema, until that closed in 1969.

The Grand Theatre

Opened on Corporation Street in 1883 and was one of the City's largest, seating 2,200 on four levels. Owner Andrew Melville sold it to Moss Empires in 1907 who subsequently redesigned the auditorium and renamed it as the Grand Theatre of Varieties. In 1930, the building was sold to Universal Pictures, who ran it as a cinema for four years, following which it was run by Mecca as The Grand Casino Ballroom until its closure in 1963.

The Imperial Theatre, Bordesley

Opened exactly one week before the Hippodrome on 2 October 1899 as a playhouse. Four years later it was taken over by Moss Empires who refurbished the building and changed the name to Bordesley Palace, where audiences were promised "high class music and varieties". In 1913 it reverted to its role as a playhouse when the building was leased to Mr Cox who ran it for the next 13 years with a mixture of plays and melodramas. It closed in 1929 and was turned into a cinema. The building was requisitioned as a food store by the government during the war and was subsequently demolished in 1957.

New Star Theatre of Wales

Opened in 1885 in Snow Hill. Less than a year later it closed and after substantial alterations reopened as the Queen's Theatre and Opera House with a production of *The Bohemian Girl* attended by Joseph Chamberlain. By 1906 it had changed its name (and its image) again, transformed this time into the Metropole Theatre

Birmingham's lost theatres

MOOR STREET THEATRE, Moor Street
Opened 1740 Closed 1764

THE THEATRE, King Street (New Street)
Opened 1751 Closed 1779

THEATRE ROYAL, New Street
Opened 1774 Closed 1956 Demolished 1956

THE GAIETY, Coleshill Street
Opened 1846 Closed 1920 Demolished 1969

PRINCE OF WALES THEATRE, Broad Street
Opened 1856 Closed 1941 Demolished 1987

DAY'S CRYSTAL PALACE, Smallbrook Street
Opened 1862 Re-opened 1894 as The Empire Demolished 1951

LONDON MUSEUM & CONCERT HALL, Digbeth
Opened 1863 Current use: Restaurant & Karate

GRAND THEATRE, Corporation Street
Opened 1883 Closed 1930 Demolished 1963

METROPOLE THEATRE, Snow Hill
Opened 1885 Closed 1911 Demolished 1951

ASTON THEATRE ROYAL, Aston
Opened 1893 Closed 1926 Demolished 1970

THEATRE ROYAL, Smethwick
Opened 1897 Closed 1932 Demolished 1936

BORDESLEY PALACE, Bordesley
Opened 1899 Closed 1929 Demolished 1959

CARLTON THEATRE, Saltley
Opened 1900 Closed 1921 Bombed 1941

THE WINDSOR, Bearwood
Opened c1900 Current use: Snooker Hall

NEW HIPPODROME, West Bromwich
Opened 1906 Closed 1922 Demolished 1922

ASTON HIPPODROME, Aston
Opened 1908 Closed 1960 Demolished 1980

EMPIRE THEATRE, Smethwick
Opened 1910 Current use: Shop

PALACE THEATRE, Spring Hill
Opened 1911 Closed c1930 Demolished 1981

NEWTOWN PALACE, Aston
Opened 1914 Closed 1961 Demolished 1990

THE EMPIRE, West Bromwich
Opened 1914 Closed 1927 Demolished 1973

GOSTA GREEN HALL, Gosta Green
Opened 1951 Closed c1955

BIRMINGHAM THEATRE CENTRE, Islington Row
Opened 1957 Closed c1970 Demolished 1970

THEATRE ROYAL, BIRMINGHAM.

TO-NIGHT AT 7.30, AND THURSDAY MATINEE AT TWO.
GEORGE EDWARDES & CHARLES FROHMAN
Present the Great Musical Success—
"A WALTZ DREAM,"
Music by Oscar Straus.
Book by Felix Doerman and Leopold Jacobson.
Adapted for the English Stage by Basil Hood.
Lyrics by Adrian Ross.
THE STRONGEST CAST EVER SENT OUT OF LONDON.
AMY AUGARDE, JOHN HUMPHRIES,
ETHEL CADMAN, WILSON PEMBROKE,
MAY MARTON, LESLIE HOLLAND,
PEGGY LORRAINE, WILLIE WARDE, JUN.,
MARY HAMILTON, ARTHUR ROYD,
AND
MAY DE SOUSA.
FULL CHORUS. AUGMENTED ORCHESTRA.
Under the direction of Hamish MacCunn.
Produced by J. A. E. Malone.
FULL LADIES' ORCHESTRA of Sixteen Specially Selected London Concert Soloists.
No Advance in Prices. Box Office Now Open. Tel. 435 Mid.
April 26.—MR. MARTIN HARVEY. (See below.)
PROMENADE CONCERTS SEASON May 10. Box Office open to the public April 26.

THEATRE ROYAL, BIRMINGHAM.

MONDAY NEXT, for Six Nights and Thursday Matinee,
IMPORTANT ENGAGEMENT OF MR.
MARTIN HARVEY,
MISS N. DE SILVA AND COMPANY.

Monday, Tuesday Evening, and Thursday Matinee— "THE ONLY WAY."
Wednesday .... "THE LAST HEIR."
Thursday Evening.." A CIGARETTE MAKER'S ROMANCE." (Preceded by "THE CONSPIRACY.")
Friday and Saturday Evenings— "THE BREED OF THE TRESHAMS."
Box Plans Open, Dress Circle and Orchestra Stalls 5s., Balcony and Pit Stalls 4s.

PRINCE OF WALES THEATRE

BOX PLANS NOW OPEN FOR THE
Last Appearance in Birmingham Prior to his Visit to the United States of
FORBES ROBERTSON
AND HIS LONDON COMPANY,
On MONDAY NEXT, April 26, Six Nights, and MATINEE THURSDAY, in
"THE PASSING OF THE THIRD FLOOR BACK,"
By Jerome K. Jerome
(As played 200 times in London).
N.B.—A Handsome SOUVENIR containing Artistic Reproductions of Principal Characters and Scenes will be presented to those Booking Seats for MONDAY, April 26, the 250th Performance. Dress Circle and Stalls, 6s.
NOTE.—On TUESDAY, April 27, the Theatre is Exclusively Reserved for the Guests of the Lord Mayor of Birmingham.

ALEXANDRA THEATRE.—TO-DAY, at 2.30 and 7.30, "HER LIFE IN LONDON." Matinee Every Wednesday at 2.30. Box Office Open 11 till 3. 'Phone 589 Midland.

BORDESLEY PALACE THEATRE.—TO-DAY, at 2.30 and 7.30, J. A. Campbell's Company, in "THE OLD FOLKS AT HOME." Matinee Every Wednesday at 2.30.

METROPOLE THEATRE, SNOW HILL.—TO-NIGHT, at 7.30.—First Visit here of Messrs. Armitage and Leigh's Company, including William Clayton, Arthur Leigh, and Miss Bessie Rignold in the Great West End Success,
"LEAH KLESCHNA."
Box Office Open 10.30 to 5.30. 'Phone 6129 Central.

THEATRE ROYAL, ASTON.
TO-NIGHT, at 7.30,
"THE WOMAN PAYS."

EMPIRE PALACE, HURST STREET.

TWO PERFORMANCES NIGHTLY, 6.50 & 9.0 O'CLOCK.
MATINEE, THURSDAY, 2.30.

GEORGE GRAY,
Of "Fighting Parson" Fame, and Company in a New Sketch,
"PARSON GRAY, V.C."
LYRIC QUARTETTE, in Harmonised Illustrated Numbers.
PICCOLINOS, the Miniature Marvels of the World.
BELLE DAVIS and Her Pick Chick Actors.
BRONZO BROS., AMERICA'S FAMOUS JUMPERS.
FAYRE & MANNING, Comedians and Rhythmic Dancers.
LITTLE MAUDIE FRANCIS, Child Vocalist and Dancer.
AMERICAN BIOSCOPE, with New Pictures.

specialising in torrid melodramas. With such productions as *The Red Barn*, *The Grip of Iron*, *The Fatal Wedding*, *The Dangers of London* and *Monte Cristo* it is not surprising that it was locally referred to as "The Blood Tub". It closed in 1911 and subsequently reopened as a cinema.

THE NEWTOWN PALACE

Opened in Aston in 1914 as part of the Moss Empires circuit offering a combination of cinema and variety. It survived as a 2,000 seat mixed-use venue until 1961 when it was taken over by Ladbrokes as a Bingo club. It closed altogether in 1983.

THE 'OLD REP'

Having been designed and built by Barry Jackson as a home for the Pilgrim Players Repertory Company it opened in Station Street in 1913 with a production of *Twelfth Night*. Under his direction it achieved national recognition as a playhouse of the first rank. Many famous names cut their teeth at the 'Old Rep' (as it is now known), while others appeared there at the height of their fame, including Peggy Ashcroft, Richard Chamberlain, Noël Coward, Edith Evans, Albert Finney, Cedric Hardwicke, Derek Jacobi, Laurence Olivier, Donald Pleasance, Ralph Richardson and Paul Scofield.

Now owned by the City Council, it remains open for amateur and other productions. During the 1990s it has been the home base of Neal Foster's Birmingham Stage Company.

THE PRINCE OF WALES THEATRE

Opened in Broad Street in 1856 under the name of The Birmingham Music Hall. Charles Dickens appeared there in 1861 with a reading of *A Christmas Carol*. Under James Rogers' ownership, the building was enlarged and facilities for drama improved during the late 1860s. For a period in the 1930s the Prince of Wales was run in conjunction with the Theatre Royal. The theatre closed, never to reopen, after it was bombed in April 1941 and the remains of the building were demolished prior to the building of the International Convention Centre.

SUMMERHILL PALACE

Was opened in Spring Hill in 1911 by Moss Empires "showing beautiful motion pictures, illustrated song and selected variety". In the 1930s it became part of the ABC group and the live performances ceased. The building was demolished in 1981 and a factory now stands on the site.

THE THEATRE ROYAL

Opened in 1774 under the name of The New Theatre, seating about 2,000 people. Twice destroyed by fire, in 1792 and 1820, though the façade survived largely intact through both. After the 1820 rebuilding it was one of the first theatres to boast gas-lighting, and the auditorium was lit by over 20 chandeliers! Amongst the most famous regular visitors to the Theatre Royal was Admiral Lord Nelson who first came with Sir William and Lady Hamilton to see a production of *The Merry Wives of Windsor* in 1802. During the nineteenth century the Theatre Royal established itself as one of the most important playhouses outside London attracting virtually all the well-known names of the time. The theatre was completely rebuilt in 1904 and reopened with *Babes in the Wood*. The staple fare thereafter was drama, with a few musicals and the regular pantomimes. When Moss Empires took over the lease variety was added to the diet. With virtually no warning, the theatre was closed just before Christmas 1956 to make way for a new branch of Woolworths which itself was demolished 30 years later. Moss Empires had promised to replace the building, but this never materialised.

Partners on Stage

THE PEOPLE OF BIRMINGHAM have the opportunity to mount their own productions and perform on the Hippodrome's magnificent stage.

Readers of the Wednesday 16th July 1886 edition of the 'Birmingham Gazette', the morning newspaper of the day, would have seen the following advertisement:-

TONIGHT - ONLY - TONIGHT
By Special Permission of MR D'OYLY CARTE
GRAND AMATEUR PERFORMANCE OF
H.M.S. PINAFORE
In the Lecture Hall of the BIRMINGHAM INSTITUTE
Doors open 7.30pm Commence 8.00pm
Carriages at 10.30 pm
Reserved Seats 4/- Unreserved Seats 2/-

In the same newspaper they would have read that the Prime Minister, Mr Gladstone, was about to dissolve Parliament, and in the advertisement columns that Gentlemen could purchase a tailored suit for £2.18/- and for the Ladies, mink capes were on sale at £1.10/-. The 1886 production of *HMS Pinafore* marked the birth of the Birmingham Operatic Society. In the early years productions were mainly of Gilbert and Sullivan with the occasional light opera. This format continued until 1922 when *The Mikado* was the last Gilbert and Sullivan opera to be performed by the Society.

John Wells rehearses the Birmingham and Midland Operatic Society for 'Cavalcade', 1995.

Kismet, 1982

In 1916 a second society was formed called the 'Midland Amateur Operatic Society' and for eleven years there was friendly rivalry between the two. However, in 1927, the two societies amalgamated and, the Birmingham and Midland Operatic Society (BMOS) was born. The Society had a prolific output, and in 1956, put on the last musical, *Wild Violets* at the Theatre Royal before that theatre's cruel demise to developers rubble.

In 1957 the Society moved to the Hippodrome and their enthusiasm and talent is still an annual favourite on the Hippodrome's stage.

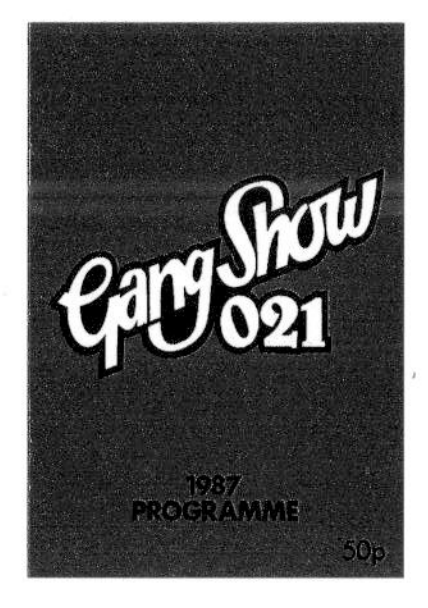

Until 1987, the County of Birmingham Scout Association presented the traditional "Gang Show" at the Hippodrome.

Productions performed at the Hippodrome by the Birmingham and Midland Operatic Society

1957	White Horse Inn
1958	Chu Chin Chow
1959	Call Me Madam
1960	South Pacific
1961	The King and I
1962	Song of Norway
1963	The Vagabond King, Gay's the Word
1964	Songs from Our Shows
1965	King's Rhapsody
1966	Carousel, Flower Drum Song
1967	The Music Man
1968	The Quaker Girl
1969	The Arcadians
1970	Oklahoma!
1971	The Merry Widow
1972	Love from Judy
1973	Hello, Dolly!
1974	The Pajama Game
1975	Show Boat
1976	The Desert Song
1977	Rose Marie
1978	The Belle of New York
1979	Annie Get Your Gun
1980	South Pacific
1981	Carousel
1982	Kismet
1983	The Merry Widow
1984	Fiddler on the Roof
1985	Hans Andersen
1986	The King and I
1987	My Fair Lady
1988	Call Me Madam
1989	The Great Waltz
1990	Oliver!
1991	Irene
1992	High Society
1993	Meet Me in St Louis
1994	42nd Street
1995	Cavalcade
1996	Oklahoma!
1997	The Sound of Music
1998	Hello, Dolly!
1999	Anything Goes

Behind The Scenes

Red Carpet Days

HRH The Princess Margaret, Countess of Snowdon, Patron of Birmingham Royal Ballet, arriving at the company's inaugural performance in 1990. Princess Margaret has been a steadfast supporter of BRB both in Birmingham and on tour.

Below: Dame Ninette de Valois arrives at Birmingham New Street Station on the new railway engine 'The Birmingham Royal Ballet' which brought the company to Birmingham in 1990.

Brian Harris

Celebrating One Hundred Years! On 9th October 1999, Mrs Frances Savage (daughter of James Draysey who built the Hippodrome in 1899) cuts the Centenary Birthday Cake in the company of Chris Kirk (Chairman of the Hippodrome Theatre Trust) and Peter Tod (Theatre Director).

HRH The Princess Royal backstage after a special 'Save The Children Fund' matinee of 'Jack and the Beanstalk', 1995.

Diana, Princess of Wales, backstage in the wardrobe department of Birmingham Royal Ballet, 1990.

'The Old Lady of Hurst Street'

1890 First edition of Ordnance Survey maps showed back to back housing covering the entire Hippodrome site.

1895 The Assembly Rooms on the corner of Hurst Street and Inge Street were erected three years before starting on the Hippodrome.

1899 Construction of the original building for Henry and James Draysey, to the design of Birmingham architect F.W. Lloyd, designed in a circus format with seating encircling the performance ring, opened 9th October 1899 and called The Tower of Varieties and Circus.

1900 Auditorium reconstructed, again to F.W. Lloyd's designs, with seating capacity reduced to 2,000 but incorporating stalls seating, dress circle, gallery and six boxes, and now named The Tivoli Theatre of Varieties.

1903 Renamed the Hippodrome, which was occasionally known as Barrasford's Hippodrome.

1924 Purchased by Moss Empires. Re-building works, after some years of closure, carried out to the design of Burdwood and Mitchell, architects, of London. Separate circle and balcony replaced with one large circle, a new stage and orchestra pit and front of house facilities extended.

1932 Construction of projection room at rear of circle.

1962 Orchestra pit lowered and new scenery dock installed.

1963 Extensive alterations to front of house carried out under the direction of Edwin M. Lawson, architect: main foyer extended and ground floor entrance introduced, new box office and stalls bars created and Hurst Street façade re-built.

1965 Moss Empires re-titled the Hippodrome, the Birmingham Theatre, but this was never really accepted by the public and in 1972 the name reverted to the Hippodrome.

1979 Birmingham City Council purchased The Hippodrome for £50,000 from Stoll Moss Theatres and leased it to the present Theatre Trust.

1981 A fifteen year programme of reconstruction, under the direction of Seymour Harris Partnership, architects of Birmingham, began with the construction of a new dressing room and stage door block in Thorp Street. Orchestra pit, band rooms, fly tower and grid rebuilt, auditorium refurbished, and stage rake removed.

1984 Former Irish Club premises above ground floor foyer altered to form The Dance Centre – space now occupied by DanceXchange.

1985 Stage and fly tower doubled in size, orchestra pit and band rooms altered, air conditioning installed in auditorium, extensive re-roofing works and alterations to front of house facilities carried out.

1986 Major improvements made to facilities for the disabled. Construction of new frontage to the Hippodrome with a grant from the last days of West Midlands County Council.

1988 Alterations to redundant envelope warehouse in Thorp Street to form new administrative offices and hospitality suites for the Hippodrome.

1990 Major construction of the purpose built accommodation for Birmingham Royal Ballet with four dance studios, changing rooms, canteen, extensive wardrobe and other support facilities.

1992 Improvement of stalls sightlines by re-raking and reconstruction of auditorium floor, seating and sound control equipment accommodation provision.

1999 Work commenced on the £28.5 million Hippodrome 2000 Development Project, a partnership between Birmingham Hippodrome, Birmingham Royal Ballet and DanceXchange, supported by The National Lottery through The Arts Council of England, Birmingham City Council, European Regional Development Fund and generous donations from the public.

List of Illustrations

Overleaf:
Sir Kenneth MacMillan's production of 'Romeo and Juliet', designed by Paul Andrews, 1992.
Photo by Bill Cooper.

4 STEPS TO HEAVEN • 42ND STREET • A CHORUS LINE • ADRIAN EDMONDSON • AD
ANNIE • ANNIE GET YOUR GUN • ANYONE FOR DENIS? • ANYTHING GOES • ARDAL O'
BARCLAY JAMES HARVEST • BARRY HUMPHRIES • BARRY WHITE • THE BEACH BOYS •
FURY • BILLY J KRAMER • BILLY OCEAN • THE BLACK AND WHITE MINSTREL SHOW •
BRUCE FORSYTH • BUBBLING BROWN SUGAR • BUD 'N' CHES • BUDDY • BUDDY RIC
CATERINA VELENTE • CATS • CAVALCADE • CHARLES AZNAVOUR • CHARLEY PRIDE •
CHESS • THE CHIEFTAINS • CHINESE MAGIC ACROBATS • THE CHIPPENDALES • CHUC
DUNN • THE COTTON CLUB • CRACKERJACK • CRAZY FOR YOU • THE DALLAS BOYS •
DIANA ROSS • DICK EMERY • DIZZY GILLESPIE • DON MACLEAN • DOOBIE BROTH
ELLINGTON • E.L.O. • EDDIE IZZARD • ELAINE PAIGE • ELECTRIC ICE WITH ROBIN
HUMPERDINCK • EVERLEY BROTHERS • EVITA • FAME • FASCINATING AIDA • FIDDLE
FOUR TOPS • FRANK SINATRA • FRANK SKINNER • FRANKIE HOWERD • FRANKIE VA
GENESIS • GEORGE BENSON • GEORGE HAMILTON • GERRY & THE PACEMAKERS •
OLD DAYS • GOODNESS GRACIOUS ME • GREASE • GREAT BALLS OF FIRE • GRIFF RH
ENFIELD • HEATWAVE • HELEN SHAPIRO • THE HEN PARTY • HENRY MANCINI • HERB
HOWARD KEEL • IGGY POP • IT AIN'T HALF HOT MUM • JAMES GALWAY • JAMES LAS
DAVIDSON • JIMMY CRICKET • JIMMY TARBUCK • JOE BROWN • JOHN COLTRANE •
JULIAN CLARY • JUNE BRONHILL • KELLY MONTEITH • KEN DODD • KENNETH BRANA
CAGE AUX FOLLES • LARRY GRAYSON • LENNY HENRY • LEO SAYER LEONARD COH
LULU • MANFRED MANN • MANHATTAN TRANSFER • MARGOT FONTEYN • MARLENE
GIRL • MICHAEL BARRYMORE • MIKE HARDING • THE MONKEES • MONTY PYTHON •
SEDAKA • NEW FACES • NIGEL KENNEDY • THE OLD MAN OF LOCHNAGAR • OLIVER!
BEAR • THE PAJAMA GAME • PAM AYRES • PAMELA STEPHENSON • PAUL DANIELS •
OPERA • PHIL COOL • PIAF • POPCORN • POSTMAN PAT • PRISONER CELL BLOCK H –
RETURN OF THE FORBIDDEN PLANET • RICHARD BRIERS • RIK MAYALL • THE ROCK
ATKINSON IN REVUE • THE ROYAL BALLET • RUBY TURNER • RUDOLPH NUREYEV •
BROTHERS • SHAKIN' STEVENS • SHOWADDYWADDY • SHOW BOAT • SIMON & GARFU
LIKE IT HOT • SONG AND DANCE • SOOTY • THE SOUND OF MUSIC • SPIKE MILLI
TANGO PASION • TEMPERANCE SEVEN CONCERT • THE TEMPTATIONS • THE THREE
BENNETT • TRIBUTE TO THE BLUES BROTHERS • VAL DOONICAN • VAN MORRIS